Kaplan Publishing are constantly find[ing] **KT-232-424** ways to make a difference to your studies and our exciting online resources really do offer something different to students looking for exam success.

This book comes with free MyKaplan online resources so that you can study anytime, anywhere. **This free online resource is not sold separately and is included in the price of the book.**

Having purchased this book, you have access to the following online study materials:

CONTENT	AAT	
	Text	Kit
Electronic version of the book	✓	✓
Progress tests with instant answers	✓	
Mock assessments online	✓	✓
Material updates	✓	✓

How to access your online resources

Kaplan Financial students will already have a MyKaplan account and these extra resources will be available to you online. You do not need to register again, as this process was completed when you enrolled. If you are having problems accessing online materials, please ask your course administrator.

If you are not studying with Kaplan and did not purchase your book via a Kaplan website, to unlock your extra online resources please go to www.mykaplan.co.uk/addabook (even if you have set up an account and registered books previously). You will then need to enter the ISBN number (on the title page and back cover) and the unique pass key number contained in the scratch panel below to gain access. You will also be required to enter additional information during this process to set up or confirm your account details.

If you purchased through Kaplan Flexible Learning or via the Kaplan Publishing website you will automatically receive an e-mail invitation to MyKaplan. Please register your details using this email to gain access to your content. If you do not receive the e-mail or book content, please contact Kaplan Publishing.

Your Code and Information

This code can only be used once for the registration of one book online. This registration and your online content will expire when the final sittings for the examinations covered by this book have taken place. Please allow one hour from the time you submit your book details for us to process your request.

Please scratch the film to access your MyKaplan code.

Please be aware that this code is case-sensitive and you will need to include the dashes within the passcode, but not when entering the ISBN. For further technical support, please visit www.MyKaplan.co.uk

AAT

AQ2016

PROFESSIONAL DIPLOMA IN ACCOUNTING

Synoptic Assessment 2018

FAMILIARISATION AND PRACTICE KIT – BONANZA PLC

This practice kit supports study for the following AAT qualifications:
AAT Professional Diploma in Accounting – Level 4
AAT Level 4 Diploma in Business Skills
AAT Professional Diploma in Accounting at SCQF – Level 8

KAPLAN

PUBLISHING

British Library Cataloguing-in-Publication Data

A catalogue record for this book is available from the British Library.

Published by:

Kaplan Publishing UK

Unit 2 The Business Centre

Molly Millar's Lane

Wokingham

Berkshire

RG41 2QZ

ISBN: 978-1-78740-297-3

© Kaplan Financial Limited, 2018

Printed and bound in Great Britain.

This Product includes content from the International Ethics Standards Board for Accountants (IESBA), published by the International Federation of Accountants (IFAC) in 2015 and is used with permission of IFAC.

CONTENTS

Live assessment pre-release material

This practice kit is based on the live assessment pre-release information for Bonanza PLC. Make sure you download and print a copy from the AAT website to use in conjunction with this kit.

Studying this material will encourage you to think about the assessment topics in an integrated way, which is necessary for performing well in the synoptic assessment.

Note: Kaplan authors have invented scenarios and additional details when writing questions based on Bonanza. When sitting the live assessment, make sure you don't confuse what content is in the pre-release information and what additional details are in this practice kit.

You will find a wealth of other resources to help you with your studies on the AAT website:

www.aat.org.uk/

Quality and accuracy are of the utmost importance to us so if you spot an error in any of our products, please send an email to mykaplanreporting@kaplan.com with full details, or follow the link to the feedback form in MyKaplan.

Our Quality Co-ordinator will work with our technical team to verify the error and take action to ensure it is corrected in future editions.

SYNOPTIC ASSESSMENT

AAT AQ16 introduces a Synoptic Assessment, which students must complete if they are to achieve the appropriate qualification upon completion of a qualification. In the case of the Advanced Diploma in Accounting, students must pass all of the mandatory assessments and the Synoptic Assessment to achieve the qualification.

As a Synoptic Assessment is attempted following completion of individual units, it draws upon knowledge and understanding from those units. It may be appropriate for students to retain their study materials for individual units until they have successfully completed the Synoptic Assessment for that qualification.

Four units within the Professional Diploma in Accounting are mandatory. Of these, three are assessed individually in end of unit assessments, but this qualification also includes a synoptic assessment, sat towards the end of the qualification, which draws on and assesses knowledge and understanding from all four mandatory units:

- Financial statements of Limited Companies – end of unit assessment

- Management Accounting: Budgeting – end of unit assessment

- Management Accounting: Decision and Control – end of unit assessment

- Accounting Systems and Controls – assessed within the synoptic assessment only

Summary of learning outcomes from underlying units which are assessed in the synoptic assessment

Underlying unit	Learning outcomes required
Accounting Systems and Controls	LO1, LO2, LO3, LO4
Financial Statements of Limited Companies	LO1, LO5
Management Accounting: Budgeting	LO3
Management Accounting: Decision and Control	LO1, LO2, LO4, LO5

KAPLAN PUBLISHING

FORMAT OF THE ASSESSMENT

The specimen synoptic assessment comprises six tasks and covers all six assessment objectives. Students will be assessed by computer-based assessment. Marking of the assessment is partially by computer and partially human marked.

In any one assessment, students may not be assessed on all content, or on the full depth or breadth of a piece of content. The content assessed may change over time to ensure validity of assessment, but all assessment criteria will be tested over time.

The following weighting is based upon the AAT Qualification Specification documentation which may be subject to variation.

	Assessment objective	Weighting
AO1	Demonstrate an understanding of the roles and responsibilities of the accounting function within an organisation and examine ways of preventing and detecting fraud and systemic weaknesses.	20%
AO2	Evaluate budgetary reporting; its effectiveness in controlling and improving organisational performance.	15%
AO3	Evaluate an organisation's accounting control systems and procedures.	15%
AO4	Analyse an organisation's decision making and control using management accounting tools.	15%
AO5	Analyse an organisation's decision making and control using ratio analysis.	20%
AO6	Analyse the internal controls of an organisation and make recommendations.	15%
	Total	100%

Time allowed : 3 hours

PASS MARK: The pass mark for all AAT assessments is 70%.

 Always keep your eye on the clock and make sure you attempt all questions!

The detailed syllabus and study guide written by the AAT can be found at:

www.aat.org.uk/

INDEX TO QUESTIONS AND ANSWERS

EXAM TECHNIQUE

- **Do not skip any of the material** in the syllabus.

- In particular, make sure you are comfortable with **assumed knowledge** from other papers at this level and those from lower levels.

- Make sure you are **familiar** with the live assessment pre-release information and have read through it at least twice.

- **Read each question** *very* carefully.

- **Double-check your answer** before committing yourself to it.

- Answer **every** question – if you do not know an answer to a multiple choice question or true/false question, you don't lose anything by guessing. Think carefully before you **guess**.

- If you are answering a multiple-choice question, **eliminate first those answers that you know are wrong.** Then choose the most appropriate answer from those that are left.

- **Don't panic** if you realise you've answered a question incorrectly. Getting one question wrong will not mean the difference between passing and failing.

Computer-based exams – tips

- Do not attempt a CBA until you have **completed all study material** relating to it.

- On the AAT website there is a CBA demonstration. It is **ESSENTIAL** that you attempt this before your real CBA. You will become familiar with how to move around the CBA screens and the way that questions are formatted, increasing your confidence and speed in the actual exam.

- Be sure you understand how to use the **software** before you start the exam. If in doubt, ask the assessment centre staff to explain it to you.

- Questions are **displayed on the screen** and answers are entered using keyboard and mouse. At the end of the exam, in the case of those units not subject to human marking, you are given a certificate showing the result you have achieved.

- In addition to the traditional multiple-choice question type, CBAs will also contain **other types of questions**, such as number entry questions, drag and drop, true/false, pick lists or drop down menus or hybrids of these.

- In some CBAs you will have to type in complete computations or written answers.

- You need to be sure you **know how to answer questions** of this type before you sit the exam, through practice.

KAPLAN PUBLISHING

KAPLAN'S RECOMMENDED REVISION APPROACH

QUESTION PRACTICE IS THE KEY TO SUCCESS

Success in professional examinations relies upon you acquiring a firm grasp of the required knowledge at the tuition phase. In order to be able to do the questions, knowledge is essential.

However, the difference between success and failure often hinges on your exam technique on the day and making the most of the revision phase of your studies.

The **Kaplan Study Text** is the starting point, designed to provide the underpinning knowledge to tackle all questions. However, in the revision phase, poring over text books is not the answer.

Kaplan Pocket Notes are designed to help you quickly revise a topic area; however you then need to practise questions. There is a need to progress to exam style questions as soon as possible, and to tie your exam technique and technical knowledge together.

The importance of question practice cannot be over-emphasised.

The recommended approach below is designed by expert tutors in the field, in conjunction with their knowledge of the examiner and the specimen assessment.

You need to practise as many questions as possible in the time you have left.

OUR AIM

Our aim is to get you to the stage where you can attempt exam questions confidently, to time, in a closed book environment, with no supplementary help (i.e. to simulate the real examination experience).

Practising your exam technique is also vitally important for you to assess your progress and identify areas of weakness that may need more attention in the final run up to the examination.

In order to achieve this we recognise that initially you may feel the need to practice some questions with open book help.

Good exam technique is vital.

THE KAPLAN REVISION PLAN

Stage 1: Assess areas of strengths and weaknesses

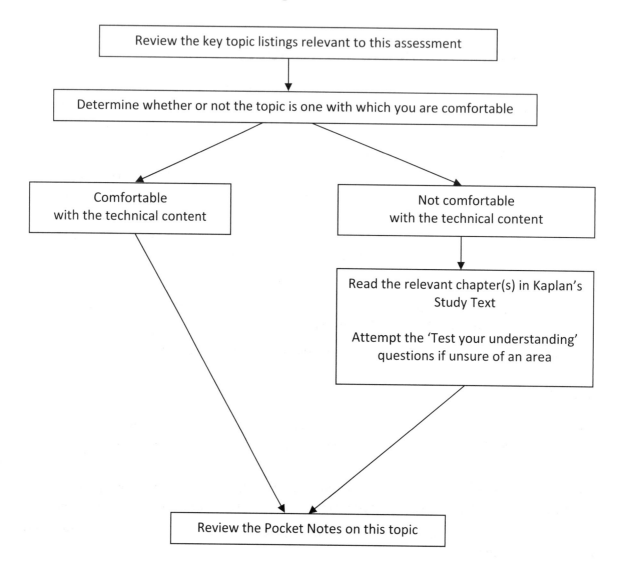

Stage 2: Familiarisation and practice questions

Follow the order of revision of topics as presented in this practice kit and attempt the questions in the order suggested.

Try to avoid referring to Study Texts and your notes and the model answer until you have completed your attempt.

Review your attempt with the model answer and assess how much of the answer you achieved.

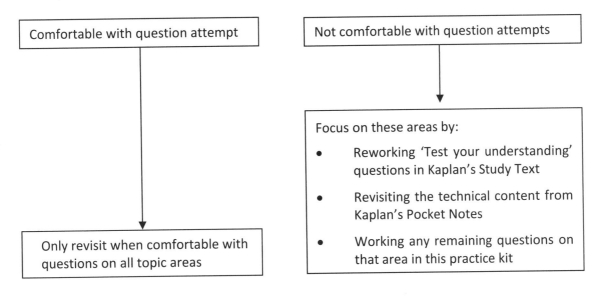

Stage 3: Final pre-exam revision

We recommend that you **attempt at least one mock examination** containing a set of previously unseen exam-standard questions based on the live assessment pre-release information.

Attempt the mock CBA online in timed, closed book conditions to simulate the real exam experience.

Also ensure that you have worked through the two sample assessments carefully and thought how to answer the same questions from the perspective of the company in the live pre-seen release.

Section 1

COMMENTARY ON LIVE PRE-RELEASE INFORMATION

1 ADVANCED PRE-RELEASE INFORMATION

COMPANY BACKGROUND AND HISTORY

Bonanza PLC is engaged in the design, development, manufacture and distribution of model railway products, toy cars and board games.

The company was set up fifty years ago by the Tennison family and became listed on the London Stock Exchange in 20X0.

Judith King, Managing Director, joined Bonanza PLC mid-way through 20X5. Judith has extensive financial and managerial experience working for both PLCs and private limited companies. She also has a strong track record in improving the performance of companies that are experiencing financial difficulties. The other directors have all previously worked within the manufacturing and retail sectors at a senior level.

Bonanza PLC offers its products under three well-known brands: Bonanza (model railways), Robit (toy cars), and Probe (board games).

These are sold through the company's website and by independent stores and major retailers throughout the United Kingdom (UK) and overseas. 75% of the company's sales are to UK customers where the brand names have an iconic status. Bonanza PLC has one major competitor in both the model railway and toy car markets – primarily due to the strength of the company's brands which make market entry costs highly prohibitive – and several smaller competitors in the board games market.

Bonanza PLC's head office, manufacturing plant and distribution warehouse are all located in London. The model railway products and toy cars are manufactured by Bonanza PLC in the UK, but the board games are produced by a third party supplier located in India. These are then shipped back to the UK for onward distribution. In recent years the product range of the company has expanded significantly, with over 1,600 product lines now actively being managed.

COMPANY PERFORMANCE

Bonanza PLC has faced challenging trading conditions over the last couple of years. This is primarily due to a downturn in the global macro-economic environment in which the company operates and increased competition from the video games sector. Consumers have less money to spend on their hobbies and toys and there is a greater number of competing interests for this. Companies operating in the video games sector also typically have far higher marketing budgets than Bonanza PLC can afford.

Bonanza PLC's difficulties have also been compounded by supply chain and warehousing issues. The company does not enjoy an exclusive relationship with its Indian supplier, and this has led to delays in introducing new products and meeting existing demand, as the supplier also has to satisfy the needs of other customers and only has a limited manufacturing capacity. There have also been problems with the stock control process in the UK warehouse, with high levels of stock building up for some product lines and stock-outs for others. This has had an adverse impact on customer goodwill and a potentially harmful effect on the reputation of the brands upon which Bonanza PLC greatly relies.

Bonanza PLC reported lower revenues and profits for the year ending 31 December 20X4 and began to experience cash flow problems in the early part of 20X5. Ridley Nolan, the then Managing Director, resigned and was replaced by Judith King.

Upon her appointment, Judith immediately announced a major strategic review of all aspects of the business – in order to increase profits and improve cash generation – and sought additional equity funding and a revised overdraft facility to help support the working capital needs of the company and reassure creditors. Bonanza PLC has yet to go overdrawn since issuing the shares.

EMPLOYEES

Recruitment, development and retention of high quality staff are crucial to the success of any business. Bonanza PLC employs 210 people in total (Production 70, Sales, Marketing and Distribution 106, and Administration 34). A number of designers and skilled craftsmen work in the Production department, which enables Bonanza PLC to continually release innovative new products to the market. This allows them to remain contemporary and stay ahead of the competition, which is essential to preserve the status of its brands. Although Bonanza PLC has continued to hire experienced professionals, it has had to cut its apprenticeship programme and curtail spending on certain training courses in order to save costs. The number of people employed in Sales, marketing and distribution has also fallen in recent years as the company has expanded its e-commerce platform.

Upon joining the company Judith King immediately implemented an annual UK employee survey to ascertain how Bonanza PLC's employees felt about all aspects of their work, including levels of workload, fair treatment in the work-place, management communications, and career path. She had used the questionnaire in the previous company she had worked for and found that it led to year-on-year improvement and a more positive and inclusive working environment. Staff turnover rates and levels of absenteeism have been markedly higher for Bonanza PLC since the company first began to experience financial difficulties, and the survey confirmed that staff morale was poor, with many employees expressing concerns about their job security. An Equality and Diversity Committee has also now been set up, in response to the survey results, to build and form a culture within Bonanza PLC that values difference in the workplace.

CUSTOMERS

Customer loyalty, as measured by the number of repeat sales made to customers, reached a low point in the first six months of the year. As a consequence Bonanza PLC has initiated an action plan to engage more with customers, principally through social media, for example discussion forums and blogs, and improve levels of customer service. Judith King believes that taking account of what customers think and how they feel will increase their sense of inclusion and thereby increase sales.

Given that a higher proportion of Bonanza PLC's sales are now being made direct to customers through its website – following a decrease in the number of retail outlets selling their product on the high street – the company has also increased investment in its e-commerce operations to help ensure a smooth and positive customer experience.

STAFF

Some of Bonanza PLC's key personnel are listed below:

Managing Director	Judith King
Finance Director	Chris Burke
Production Director	Lech Polaski
Sales Director	Tanisha Prince
Chief Accountant	Harry Archer
Purchasing Manager	Sheila Atim
Warehouse Manager	Bertie Carvel
Credit Controller	Kumail Sharif
Accounts Payable Clerk	Jemma May
Accounts Receivable Clerk	Robert Dobson
General Accounts Clerk and Cashier	Laura Wood
Payroll Clerk	John Mann

BONANZA PLC'S FINANCIAL STATEMENTS

The financial statements of Bonanza PLC for the year ended 31 December 20X5 show that the company had a turnover of £62 million, and made a profit before tax of £2.2 million.

BONANZA PLC – STATEMENT OF PROFIT OR LOSS FOR THE Y/E 31 DECEMBER 20X5

Continuing operations	£000
Revenue	**62,000**
Cost of sales	(33,874)
Gross profit	28,126
Distribution costs	(15,922)
Administrative expenses	(9,634)
Profit from operations	**2,570**
Finance costs	(351)
Profit before tax	2,219
Tax	(427)
Profit for the period from continuing operations	**1,792**

BONANZA PLC – STATEMENT OF FINANCIAL POSITION AS AT 31 DECEMBER 20X5

	£000
ASSETS	
Non-current assets	
Property and equipment	6,718
Current assets	
Inventories	7,916
Trade receivables	11,465
Cash and cash equivalents	1,470
	20,851
Total assets	27,569
EQUITY AND LIABILITIES	
Equity	
Ordinary share capital (£1 shares)	1,000
Share premium	12,486
Retained earnings	4,651
Total equity	18,137
Non-current liabilities	
Bank loans	2,168
Current liabilities	
Trade payables	6,849
Tax liabilities	415
	7,264
Total liabilities	9,432
Total equity and liabilities	27,569

2 ANALYSIS AND COMMENTARY

A key question is how best to assess the pre-release information.

The simplest approach is to read through each section and ask yourself what this is telling you about the company, focussing on control issues and the effectiveness of its systems and processes.

Let us take each section in turn:

COMPANY BACKGROUND AND HISTORY

Key aspects from this section are as follows:

- Bonanza designs, develops, manufactures and distributes toys under three iconic brands - Bonanza (model railways), Robit (toy cars), and Probe (board games).

  > Note: In many respects this company looks a lot like Hornby
  >
  > Hornby has 5 main product areas – model trains (Hornby), slot cars (Scalextric), plastic models (Airfix), collectable models (Corgi) and paints (Humbro).

- Each of the 4 stages of design, development, manufacture and distribution will have different control challenges.

- Bonanza sells via independent shops, major retailers and its website, both within the UK and overseas.

- The number of product lines has expanded rapidly and it may be that some rationalisation of product lines is needed to give better focus.

COMPANY PERFORMANCE

Bonanza has faced challenging trading conditions over the last couple of years meaning that cost control is even more important in achieving the company's objectives.

Bonanza's difficulties have been compounded by supply chain and warehousing issues so make sure you can discuss both purchasing and inventory controls and systems.

Furthermore, the company has had cash flow problems, so controls regarding the cash cycles and also credit management are critical.

EMPLOYEES

Recruitment, development and retention of high quality staff are crucial to Bonanza's success. However, these are at risk due to cutting the apprenticeship scheme and reducing training costs. Mistakes are thus more likely to occur, emphasising the need for adequate controls to prevent and detect the errors.

High staff turnover and low morale also increases the risk of fraud and theft, again stressing the need for adequate controls to reduce this risk.

CUSTOMERS

We are told that customer loyalty is at an all-time low so Bonanza needs to review both product quality and customer service. For example does the company have adequate controls to ensure that the correct goods are despatched swiftly to the right customer when sales are made via the website?

STAFF

A list of key staff help you see how the organisation is structured and also if there are obvious control issues relating to responsibilities – for example, having a separate Accounts Payable Clerk and Accounts Receivable Clerk should mean better segregation of duties.

GPL'S FINANCIAL STATEMENTS

You could calculate ratios to see if any key problems are highlighted:

	(Working)	Ratio
Gross margin (%)	28,126/62,000	45.4%
Operational margin (%)	2,570/62,000	4.1%
ROCE (%)	2,570/(18,137 + 2,168)	12.7%
Current ratio	20,851/7,264	2.9:1
Quick ratio	(20,851 – 7,916)/7,264	1.8:1
Inventory days	(7,916/33,864) × 365	85 days
Receivables days	(11,465/62,000) × 365	67 days
Payables days	(6,849/33,864) × 365	74 days
Operating cycle	85 + 67 – 74	78 days
Gearing (Debt/Equity)	2,168/18,137	0.12×

The effectiveness of such an exercise is limited by the fact that we only have one year of results and no industry averages, so have no basis of comparison to evaluate figures.

Furthermore it is likely that Bonanza's demand is seasonal with additional sales in the run up to Christmas. As a result a December year end could mean that the inventory levels given are lower than average but receivables and payables may be higher than is typical

Given all this, we can make the following comments:

- Gross margin is good, indicating that the combination of brand names and sales channels is working.

- However, the operating profit margin seem low, possibly indicating a need to review areas such as distribution costs and administration to see if there are cost inefficiencies or control issues.

- Overall, ROCE seems low, which may not be acceptable to external shareholders.

- It could be argued that there is no real concerns over short term liquidity risk as both current and quick ratios are greater than 1. However, this view is countered by the relatively long operating cycle. A long operating cycle will increase the risk of overtrading as more funds are tied up in working capital.

- Inventory days at 85 days are excessively high and increase the risk of obsolescence as customer tastes change. The situation is even worse than the average figures indicate as the year-end figure may be lower than what is typical due to seasonal demand, and we are told that stock levels for some lines are too low, resulting in stock-outs, meaning that the holding period for some lines must be higher than 85.

- We are not told the split between cash sales (presumably most customers via the website) and credit sales (presumably to independent shops). However, the receivables days seems high at an average of 67 days. This could indicate credit control problems, even given the seasonality aspect mentioned above.

- Payables days also seem high, although this could be unrepresentative due to seasonal trade. However, is there a danger that we are at risk of upsetting suppliers, which could result in delays in delivery or poor quality, both of which could seriously compromise Bonanza's plans to introduce new products on a regular basis?

- Financial gearing is low, so there should be scope to raise debt finance for new projects if required.

WHAT NEXT?

You do not need to learn any of the above analysis – the aim is to help you feel comfortable with the company and what it does and to think about the assessment topics in an integrated way.

In some respects the main reason for looking at the pre-release material is to feel comfortable with the scenario and to know what is there so you can refer back to it if necessary.

- In sample assessment 1 all relevant information was given to you within the tasks, so there was little need to refer back to the pre-release material in order to answer them.

- However, in sample assessment 2 you needed to refer back to the financial statements in order to calculate ratios.

Section 2

PRACTICE QUESTIONS

TASK 1.1

Assessment objective 1	Demonstrate an understanding of the roles and responsibilities of the accounting function within an organisation and examine ways of preventing and detecting fraud and systemic weaknesses.

1 STATUTORY DUTY

Who has the statutory duty to prepare accounts for Bonanza?

The company auditors.	
The directors of the company.	
Chris Burke, Finance Director.	
Harry Archer, Chief Accountant.	
Companies House.	

2 RESPONSIBILITY

Who is responsible for maintaining sound risk management and internal control systems within Bonanza?

The company auditors.	
The directors of the company.	
Chris Burke, Finance Director.	
Harry Archer, Chief Accountant.	
Companies House.	

3 BANK RECONCILIATION 1

You are assisting with the month-end bank reconciliation at Bonanza.

The bank statement has been compared with the cash book and the following differences identified:

1 Cheques totalling £1,629 paid into the bank at the end of the month are not showing on the bank statement.

2 Bank interest paid of £106 was not entered in the cash book.

3 A cheque for £350 written on 2 June has been incorrectly entered in the cash book at 2 May.

4 A receipt from a customer of £1,645 has cleared the bank but has not been entered in the cash book.

The balance showing on the bank statement at 31 May is a credit of £363 and the balance in the cash book is a debit of £103.

Use the following table to show the THREE adjustments you need to make to the cash book.

Adjustment	Amount £	Debit/Credit

4 BANK RECONCILIATION 2

Which of the following errors would be picked up by a bank reconciliation? (Select all that apply)

	Yes	No
A customer was accidentally invoiced twice for the same item.		
An independent retailer took a 2% prompt payment discount despite not having paid within the timescales required to earn a discount.		
Bank interest received had not been posted to the cash book.		
A payment to a supplier of £2,500 had accidentally been posted as £250.		

5 SALES LEDGER CONTROL ACCOUNT RECONCILIATION 1

You are working on the final accounts of Bonanza, which operates a manual accounting system.

You have the following information:

(a) A casting error has been made and one of the customer accounts has been undercast by £65.

(b) Sales returns totalling £280 have not been entered in a customer's individual ledger.

(c) A receipt of £1,300 from a customer has been credited to the customer's account in the sales ledger as 130.

(d) A credit sale of £3,000 (excluding VAT at 20%) has not been included in the relevant customer's account in the sales ledger.

(e) A customer account with a balance of £99 has been duplicated in the list of balances.

(f) A customer with a credit balance of £50 has been listed as a debit balance of £50.

You now need to make the appropriate adjustments in the table below.

For each adjustment clearly state the amount and whether the item should be added or subtracted from the list of balances. If no adjustment is required enter '0' into the amount column.

	Add/Subtract	£
Total from list of balances		31,100
Adjustment for (a)		
Adjustment for (b)		
Adjustment for (c)		
Adjustment for (d)		
Adjustment for (e)		
Adjustment for (f)		
Revised total to agree with SLCA		33,116

6 SALES LEDGER CONTROL ACCOUNT RECONCILIATION 2

Which of the following errors would be picked up by performing a sales ledger control account reconciliation?

	Yes	No
A customer was accidentally invoiced twice for the same item.		
An independent retailer was sold items at the wrong price.		
Credit balances had been omitted from the list of receivables balances.		
A payment from a customer of £230 had accidentally been posted as £320 to their individual account in the receivables ledger.		

7 PURCHASES LEDGER CONTROL ACCOUNT RECONCILIATION

You are working on the final accounts of Bonanza, which operates a manual accounting system.

You have the following information:

(a) A payment of £1,277 to a supplier has been debited to the supplier's account in the purchases ledger as £1,722.

(b) A supplier with a debit balance of £2,170 has been listed as a credit balance.

(c) A credit purchase return of £1,000 (net of VAT at 20%) has not been included in the relevant supplier's account in the purchase ledger.

(d) A casting error has been made and one of the supplier accounts has been overcast by £132.

(e)   A supplier account with a balance of £2,100 has been omitted from the list.

(f)   A credit purchase has been entered into the individual account net of VAT at 20%. The net amount is £600.

You now need to make the appropriate adjustments in the table below. For each adjustment clearly state the amount and whether the item should be added or subtracted from the list of balances.

	Add/Subtract	£
Total from list of balances		132,589
Adjustment for (a)		
Adjustment for (b)		
Adjustment for (c)		
Adjustment for (d)		
Adjustment for (e)		
Adjustment for (f)		
Revised total to agree with PLCA		129,582

8   ERRORS

You are working on the accounting records of Bonanza.

A trial balance has been drawn up and a suspense account opened. You need to make some corrections and adjustments for the year ended 31 December 20X6.

You may ignore VAT in this task.

Record the journal entries needed in the general ledger to deal with the items below.

(a)   Motor expenses of £4,500 have been posted to the Motor Vehicles at Cost account in error. The other side of the entry is correct.

Journal

	Dr £	Cr £

(b)   Office sundries costing £16 were paid for by cash. Only the entry to the cash account was made.

Journal

	Dr £	Cr £

(c)   No entries have been made for closing inventory as at 31 December 20X6. It has been valued at a selling price of £227,184. The sales price has had 20% added onto its original cost.

Journal

	Dr £	Cr £

(d)   Discounts allowed of £1,270 have been posted as £1,720 on both sides of the entry.

Journal

	Dr £	Cr £

9   CHANGEOVER

The Board of BONANZA are considering updating the accounting system.

Chris Burke (FD) is suggesting that the direct changeover method be adopted. However, Lech Polaski (Production Director) has argued that direct changeover is usually the highest risk alternative available.

Which TWO of the following controls can mitigate the risk of system failure during direct changeover?

Testing	
Training	
System documentation	
Data backup	
Check digits	

10   INFORMATION SYSTEM CONTROLS

Information system controls can be classified as 'security controls' and 'integrity controls'.

Drag and drop the following controls into the correct category.

	Security	Integrity
Locked doors		
Passwords		
Batch totals		
Reconciliation		
CCTV		
Check digits		
Authorisation of data entry		
Fire alarms		

11   PURCHASE CYCLE CONTROLS 1

BONANZA has experienced occasions when payment was made for goods not received.

Which TWO of the following controls in a purchase cycle could be implemented to reduce the risk of payment of goods not received?

Sequentially pre-numbered purchase requisitions and sequence check.	
Matching of goods received note with purchase invoice.	
Goods are inspected for condition and quantity and agreed to purchase order before acceptance.	
Daily update of inventory system.	

12   PURCHASE CYCLE CONTROLS 2

BONANZA has experienced occasions when unnecessary goods and services were purchased.

Which TWO of the following controls in the purchase cycle could be implemented to reduce the risk of procurement of unnecessary goods and services?

Centralised purchasing department.	
Sequentially pre-numbered purchase requisitions and sequence check.	
Orders can only be placed with suppliers from the approved suppliers list.	
All purchase requisitions are signed as authorised by an appropriate manager.	

13 EXPENSE CLAIM CONTROLS

Harry Grisham has been appointed as the new IT manager at Bonanza. Harry really enjoys the job and even though the remuneration is not great, the other managers at the company have explained the way they 'get around' that issue. The sales manager explains to Harry that the key is to 'put everything on expenses – private petrol, drinks and even clothing. It's all fine and as long as you have a receipt, no-one in the finance department will question it'. He continues that 'It's fine because the board are aware of it and turn a blind eye'.

Which ONE of the following essential internal control measures is evidently missing?

Bonanza lacks a control environment as the board are not setting an ethical tone at the top.	
Bonanza lacks an Internal Audit department.	
Bonanza lacks an experienced finance manager.	
Bonanza lacks an external auditor.	

14 PASSWORDS 1

You have been asked to set up a password for BONANZA's accounting system.

Which of the following would be the most secure?

24june1963	
LaraJo	
mypassword	
Qwerty123!#	

15 PASSWORDS 2

You have been asked to set up a new system of passwords for BONANZA's accounting system.

Which TWO of the following would reduce the effectiveness of passwords?

Requirement that passwords are changed every two weeks	
Users are allowed to choose their own passwords	
Automatic lock-out after 3 failed attempts to access system	
Making the sharing of passwords a disciplinary offence	
Displaying the password on the screen when entered	

16 INTERNAL CONTROLS 1

An internal control system in an organisation consists of five components: the control environment, the risk assessment process, the information system, control activities and monitoring of controls.

Match each of the following activities to the component that it illustrates.

	Control environment	Information system	Control activities
The process of preparing the financial statements			
Locking the inventory storeroom			

17 INTERNAL CONTROLS 2

Bonanza is looking at introducing new internal controls to help reduce the risk of fraud.

Match each of the following activities to the type of control that it illustrates.

	Authorisation	Information processing	Physical control
The financial controller will count petty cash on a weekly basis			
There will be two keys to the locked safe: one held by the FD and the other by the MD.			

18 INTERNAL CONTROLS 3

Bonanza is looking at introducing new computer controls to reduce payroll fraud. Computer controls can be described as "general" and "application".

Match each of the following activities to the type of computer control that it illustrates.

	General	Application
Storing extra copies of programs and data files off-site		
New programmes to check data fields on input transactions		
Manual checks to ensure that input data were authorised		
Password protection limiting access to data		
Range checks on payroll processing		
Manual checks to ensure that timesheets are authorised before details are processed		

19   INTERNAL CONTROLS 4

Bonanza is looking at introducing new internal controls but the directors are concerned that even the best controls still have limitations.

Indicate whether the following limitations are true or false.

	True	False
The cost of implementing controls may be more expensive than the benefits gained due to reduced risk		
The effectiveness of many controls rely on the integrity of those applying them		
Internal controls are only applied to material items so smaller items remain unchecked		
Standard controls may not be designed to deal with unusual transactions		

20   FRAUD 1

Harry Archer is concerned that some BONANZA staff may be misappropriating customer remittances.

Which THREE of the following control activities would best prevent this fraud occurring?

Segregation of duties between cash handling and recording	
Post opening by two people	
Investigation of differences between website sales and cash banked	
Regular banking of cash and cheques received in the post	

21   FRAUD 2

Given high staff turnover and low morale within Bonanza, the financial controller is worried that fictitious employees could be included on the payroll by a dishonest employee from the accounts department.

Which ONE of the following control activities would best prevent this occurring?

Payroll standing data periodically printed out and checked on a line-by-line basis to independently held employee details	
Use of hierarchical passwords over standing data files	
Pre-authorisation of all amendments to payroll standing data by an independent official	
Supervision of the wages pay out by an independent official	

TASK 1.2

Assessment objective 2	Evaluate budgetary reporting; its effectiveness in controlling and improving organisational performance.

22 TRAINING COSTS

The directors of Bonanza are concerned that training funds are not being used and focussed as well as thought. Given this, they have appointed a new training manager, Petr Higgs.

One month later, Petr received the following email from Lech Polaski (Production Director)

To: Petr Higgs, Training Manager

From: Lech Polaski

Subject: Costs out of control

I am writing to express concern over the results of your first month in charge of training.

In particular you need to explain the reasons for your cost overrun:

	Budget	Actual
Number of trainees	20	25
Fixed costs (£)	13,000	12,900
Variable costs (£)	1,000	1,200
Total cost (£)	14,000	14,100

Adverse variance £100

Please come and see me immediately.

Petr was alarmed by the email as he didn't even know there was going to be a performance appraisal of this kind and certainly hadn't been involved in any budgeting or target setting.

He was also concerned that there seemed to be no mention of how good the training was.

(a) **BRIEFLY discuss THREE weaknesses in the above use of performance reports to improve the focus of training within Bonanza.** **(9 marks)**

Weakness 1

Weakness 2

Weakness 3

(b)   Outline THREE performance indicators that could be used to assess the quality of the training provided. **(6 marks)**

Performance Indicator 1

Performance Indicator 2

Performance Indicator 3

(Total 15 marks)

23 BUDGETING

Dave Smith, one of the sales managers working for Tanisha Price (Sales Director) has presented a budget proposal for the board games side of the business for 20X6 for approval by the Board of Bonanza. Harry Archer (Chief Accountant) has already completed some analysis of the budget by adding additional KPIs at looking at comparatives. Unfortunately he is currently ill, so you have been asked to comment on the proposal.

Budget

	Actual 20X5	Budget 20X6	% change
Sales volume (000s of games)	80	88	10.0%
	£000	£000	
Sales revenue	28,000	30,240	8.0%
Cost of sales	(14,500)	(15,515)	7.0%
Gross profit	**13,500**	**14,725**	
Selling and distribution costs	(8,000)	(7,896)	(1.3%)
Administration costs	(4,000)	(3,300)	(17.5%)
Operating profit	**1,500**	**3,529**	
Gross profit margin	48.2%	48.7%	

Notes:

- Bonanza plan to release five new board games in 20X6 and won an industry award for 'Best Family Board Game' in 20X5.

- The value of the GBP (£) is expected to strengthen against the Indian Rupee in 20X6 , meaning that imports should be less expensive.

Comparative data for games and toys

	Bonanza Actual 20X5	Industry Forecast 20X6
Growth in sales volume	7.0%	5.0%
Gross profit margin	45.4%	28.0%

Evaluate the Board Game budget for 20X6 by reference to the following assumed (or implied) growth rates and margins. In your answer discuss whether or not you feel the figures are realistic and why.
                                                                    (15 marks)

Figure	Whether or not realistic
Sales volume growth of 10.0%	
Sales revenue growth of 8.0%	
Cost of sales growth of 7.0%	
Gross margin of 48.7%	
Fall in selling costs of 1.3%	
Fall in administration costs of 17.5%	

Conclusion – whether or not the budget is realistic

24 BONANZA BUDGETING PROCESS

Bonanza is about to undertake the next annual budgeting cycle. The different managers involved have been provided with guidance notes to help them with this.

Bonanza Budgeting Guidance (extracts)

Inflation:

Inflation should be allowed for when appropriate. For wages, rent costs and materials costs inflation, shop managers can select between the RPI (retail price index) and the CPI (consumer price index which excludes mortgage payments). Both these indexes measure past inflation in the United Kingdom where Bonanza is based.

No guidance is given about inflation of other costs.

Marketing:

The overall marketing budget is set by head office without consultation with other sales managers. Bonanza has sales managers who have responsibility for different products, markets and customers – for example, Gill Evans works with two major retailers within the UK, whereas Jenni Black is responsible for website sales.

Each year the total marketing budget is set, taking account of the specific products that Bonanza wishes to promote. No account is taken of the previous year's spend. However, it is up the other sales managers to then estimate what effect this marketing spend might have on their areas of interest.

The marketing department provide sales trend analysis based on regression analysis, which produces a straight-line relationship between the marketing spend and sales volumes for previous periods.

Provide a 'SWOT' analysis of the above budget process and recommend, where appropriate changes to this process. **(15 marks)**

Note:

A 'strength' is where you feel the process is good and a 'weakness' is where you feel the process is not so good. An 'opportunity' to improve the process may exist in places and a 'threat' is best written as a bad consequence of a poor budget process.

Strengths

Weaknesses

Opportunities

Threats

TASK 1.3

Assessment objective 3	Evaluate an organisation's accounting control systems and procedures.

Note: in the two sample assessments task 1.3 only asked for weaknesses and explanations of implications. In the two tasks here, we have also asked for recommendations as this is also useful practice for task 6.

25 BONANZA'S PURCHASING SYSTEM

Below is a description of the purchasing and payments system for Bonanza in respect of manufacturing costs in its factory.

Ordering

Whenever new materials are required, such as metal to make model railway products, the relevant department within the factory sends a requisition form to the ordering department. An order clerk raises a purchase order and contacts a number of suppliers to see which can despatch the goods first. This supplier is then chosen. The order clerk sends out the purchase order. This is not sequentially numbered and only orders above £1,000 require authorisation.

Bookkeeping

Purchase invoices are input daily by the purchase ledger clerk, who has been in the role for many years and, as an experienced team member, he does not apply any application controls over the input process. Every week the purchase day book automatically updates the purchase ledger, the purchase ledger is then posted manually to the general ledger by the purchase ledger clerk.

Payments

Bonanza maintains a current account and a number of saving (deposit) accounts. The current account is reconciled weekly but the saving (deposit) accounts are only reconciled every two months.

In order to maximise their cash and bank balance, Bonanza has a policy of delaying payments to all suppliers for as long as possible. Suppliers are paid by a bank transfer. The finance director is given the total amount of the payments list, which he authorises and then processes the bank payments.

Required:

Identify and explain FOUR deficiencies in the system, explain the possible implication of each deficiency and provide a recommendation to address each deficiency. (15 marks)

Weakness	Implication	Recommendation

26 BONANZA'S SALES AND INVENTORY PROCESSES

Bonanza's website allows individuals to order toys and games directly, and full payment is taken in advance. Currently the website is not integrated into the inventory system and inventory levels are not checked at the time when orders are placed.

Goods are despatched via local couriers; however, they do not always record customer signatures as proof that the customer has received the goods. Over the past 12 months there have been customer complaints about the delay between sales orders and receipt of goods. Bonanza has investigated these and found that, in each case, the sales order had been entered into the sales system correctly but was not forwarded to the despatch department for fulfilling.

Bonanza also has some business customers – mainly toy shops - who undergo credit checks prior to being accepted and credit limits are set accordingly by sales ledger clerks. These customers place their orders through one of the sales team, who decides on sales discount levels.

Materials are purchased from a wide range of suppliers. As a result of staff changes in the purchase ledger department, supplier statement reconciliations are no longer performed. Additionally, changes to supplier details in the purchase ledger master file can be undertaken by purchase ledger clerks as well as supervisors.

In the past six months Bonanza has changed part of its warehousing process and as a result some new equipment has been purchased, however, there are considerable levels of equipment that are now surplus to requirement. Purchase requisitions for all new equipment have been authorised by warehouse supervisors and little has been done to reduce the surplus of old equipment.

Required:

In respect of the internal control of Bonanza's sales and inventory processes, identify FIVE deficiencies, explain the possible implication of each deficiency and recommend a control to address each of these deficiencies. **(15 marks)**

Weakness	Implication	Recommendation

Weakness	Implication	Recommendation

27   BONANZA'S INVENTORY COUNTING PROCESSES

Each winter, Bonanza is obliged to count its inventory in its factory and distribution warehouse.

This year Bonanza arranged for an internal auditor to attend some of the inventory counts and feedback their findings. It was hoped that this would lead to improved procedures in the future. In one location within the factory, the local staff were short numbered and so the internal auditor acted as a counter and an auditor at the same time.

In the warehouse, pre-printed inventory sheets were produced which showed the designated bin location of all inventory lines and the staff were instructed to record the number of items that they found of each inventory line in each location.

The warehouse was split into 8 zones with two teams being responsible for 3 zones each and then, depending on how fast each team counted the other two zones could be dealt with.

Suppliers were requested not to deliver during the centralised warehouse counts. This policy was mostly followed but one supplier of rubber tyres for model toys failed to obey and a large delivery was made. The driver offloaded the stock in the car park and left so as not to interfere with the counting process.

During the count, large boxes of board games not yet unpacked were not opened but the slips on the side of the boxes were used to note the contents on the inventory sheets.

A note was made of damaged items but, since the chief accountant had already done a slow-moving inventory calculation (see task 6 for the details), old inventory was not recorded.

Outline 5 weaknesses and their effect on the accounting systems in the boxes below:
(15 marks)

Weakness	Effect of Weakness

Weakness	Effect of Weakness

TASK 1.4

Assessment objective 4	Analyse an organisation's decision making and control using management accounting tools.

28   PRODUCTION DECISIONS

Each year one of the key challenges facing Bonanza is the extent to which new models of toy cars are designed, manufactured and sold. Typically new models will be made to imitate the racing cars of the top teams in Formula 1 and World Rally Sport, along with some to copy cars seen in popular children's' television programmes and films. Linked to this, a decision must be made whether to discontinue older models.

All toy cars are manufactured using the same two production lines in the London factory. Each model must be made in batches and changing models involves extensive resetting of the machinery. Finishing the cars to the required quality is very labour intensive and the availability of this skilled labour represents a significant capacity constraint for Bonanza. This effectively means that each month a decision must be made over which cars to produce.

At the latest Board meeting there was disagreement how best to make these decisions.

The following table provided shows the sales and profitability of four potential car models for the forthcoming month.

Sales and profitability data

Car model	A	B	C	D
Potential sales demand (units)	2,500	3,000	2,000	4,000
	£	£	£	£
Selling price	15.00	12.00	12.50	10.00
Variable costs	10.00	8.00	7.00	5.00
Contribution per unit	**5.00**	**4.00**	**5.50**	**5.00**
Total contribution	12,500	12,000	11,000	20,000
Apportioned fixed overheads	(5,000)	(6,000)	(4,000)	(8,000)
Operating profit	**7,500**	**6,000**	**7,000**	**12,000**
Skilled labour time per unit (minutes)	10	9.6	12	11
Contribution per minute	**0.50**	**0.42**	**0.46**	**0.45**

Notes:

1   Discounts have been excluded from the above selling prices.

2   Fixed overheads relate to costs associated with ordering, distribution and central warehouse costs. These are apportioned on a unit basis.

Directors' discussion

At the Board meeting, the directors of Bonanza gave their views as to which of the four cars to make next month.

Judith King, the Managing Director, argued that, based on total operating profits, car D should be stocked. Her argument was that the apportioned fixed overhead had to be taken into account as it had to be covered somewhere in the business.

Tanisha Prince, the Sales Director, disagreed. Her opinion was that the allocated fixed costs were irrelevant and that they should just look at the contribution, although she was unclear whether it was better to look at contribution per unit (and pick C) or total contribution (and pick D).

Lech Polaski, the Production Director, thought the correct approach was to look at the contribution per minute as they had limited skilled labour, rather than the total or unit contribution. He thus favoured stocking car A.

(a) BRIEFLY discuss the validity of each of the three directors' views on how the final decision should be made as to which cars to stock. (9 marks)

Managing Director

Sales Director

Production Director

(b) BRIEFLY explain TWO other factors should be taken into consideration before making a final decision. (6 marks)

Factor 1

Factor 2

29   NEW SUPPLIERS

Bonanza is considering extending the range of suppliers it uses for manufacturing board games and has short-listed three potential candidates.

The decision is to be based on a range of factors, both financial and non-financial.

The financial argument will be based simply on cost. Bonanza is keen to introduce target costing to achieve a minimum 40% mark up and it is felt that suppliers should be chosen that help Bonanza achieve this.

Non-financial factors will focus on quality – both that of the product offered and the quality of the service provided.

To help collect information for making the decision, one of the most popular games, "Escape from the Island", will be used as an example. The game includes a fold out board, playing cards and character pieces. The current supplier produces a laminated game board, high gloss cards and polished wooden character pieces.

(a)   **Which of the following prices should be used for target costing?**   **(2 marks)**

The budgeted price that Bonanza has set for 20X6	
The existing price that Bonanza uses	
The market average price	
The price charged by Bonanza's main competitor for a similar game	

(b)   **Calculate the target cost for the "Escape from the Island" game using the information below.**   **(3 marks)**

Cost per unit	£
Production cost (charged by supplier)	
Transportation costs (paid by Bonanza)	2.50
Total cost	
Mark up (40%)	
Target selling price	25.20

(c) Briefly explain how the concept of value analysis applies to Bonanza and the options available to it to close any cost gap. **(4 marks)**

Value analysis
Options available to Bonanza

(d) Information for three potential suppliers of the game is given as follows:

Supplier	A	B	C
Production cost	£16.50	£15.40	£15.00
Offers price discounts for bulk orders	Yes	No	No
Typical delivery time (weeks)	3	4	7
Typical credit terms (days)	30	60	45
Playing board laminated	Yes	Yes	No
Material used for character pieces	Metal	Wood	Plastic

Discuss which supplier should be chosen by referring to both financial and non-financial factors.

(6 marks)

Financial factors

Non-financial factors

30 BONANZA TOY TRAIN PLANNING

The sales of one of Bonanza's model train ranges - a set based on steam trains of the 1940s – has been in steady decline and questions are being raised about its long-term future.

The train locomotive (engine) is packaged in a special presentation box, retailing at £50 and Bonanza makes a margin on sales of 40% on this product. This margin only accounts for variable costs. If fixed costs are averaged over all products than this product's share would be £20,000. It is not thought that there is any directly attributable fixed cost.

The reason for the decline is thought to be technology. Children are used to playing exciting games on computers snd mobile devices and so expect more excitement from other toys. Unfortunately older children no longer feel that model railways give this.

To help assess the decision to discontinue the range, data has been gathered by the sales team on the volume of sales of the engines concerned over the past two years split by quarters (8 quarters in total) and your help is being requested to provide interpretation of that data.

The data analysis was performed using regression techniques where:

$$Y = a + bX$$

Y is the sales volume and X is the relevant quarter number

The data started with quarter 1 in 2017 (Q = 1) and provided six quarters of data (up to Q = 6). The '*b*' value was found to be −50 and the '*a*' value was 1,480 units

Independent retailers have been consulted and they have said that they would be willing to continue to sell the range until at least quarter 2 of 2019.

(a)   **Using the data above complete the following table:**   **(7 marks)**

Quarter Number	Volume units	Revenue £	Variable Cost £	Contribution £
1 (Q1 2017)	1,430			
2 (Q2 2017)	1,390			
3 (Q3 2017)	1,330			
4 (Q4 2017)	1,290			
5 (Q1 2018)	1,230			
6 (Q2 2018)	1,190			
7 (Q3 2018)				
8 (Q4 2018)				
9 (Q1 2019)				
10 (Q2 2019)				

(b)   **Briefly discuss the meaning of the value 'b' above and your findings using the data and comment on whether Bonanza, from a financial viewpoint, would want to continue to supply this product up to and including quarter 2 2019   (6 marks)**

(c) Briefly discuss any non-financial considerations regarding the withdrawal of a particular range from sale. **(2 marks)**

TASK 1.5

Assessment objective 5	Analyse an organisation's decision making and control using ratio analysis.

31 BONANZA AND OVERTRADING

Harry Archer has expressed concerns that Bonanza's future growth rate (10% growth in revenue expected for 20X6) may result in an overtrading position, where its financial and other resources are insufficient for the rate of expansion.

To help assess the extent of this risk a range of ratios have been calculated to create a scorecard based on Bonanza's forecast performance for 20X6.

These are given below, together with some ratios from 20X5.

(a) Complete the scorecard by calculating the missing ratios. **(10 marks)**

BONANZA Scorecard	Y/e 31/12/X6	Y/e 31/12/X5
Profitability and gearing		
Gross profit %	38.4%	45.4%
Operating profit %	3.6%	%
Return on capital employed	11.5%	%
Gearing (debt/equity)	0.20×	0.12×
Liquidity ratios		
Current ratio	3.8:1	2.9:1
Acid test/Quick ratio	2.4:1	:1
Working capital days		
Inventory holding period	70 days	days
Trade receivables collection period	71 days	67 days
Trade payables payment period	60 days	74 days
Working capital cycle	81 days	days

(b) Select the **ONE** correct observation about each aspect of business performance below. **(10 marks)**

Profitability

20X6 will be a year of steady, if unspectacular, progress. Although margins have dipped, the return on capital employed has been kept constant.	
The changes in gross margin could be due to cost control problems concerning distribution.	
Increased competition and the resulting pressure on prices could explain the change in each of the three profitability ratios.	

Gearing

The increased gearing ratio proves that Bonanza has no problems raising additional debt finance.	
It is likely that the interest cover ratio has increased.	
The increased gearing ratio shows that the shareholders' position has become more risky.	

Liquidity

Both ratios have increased, which indicates that the company is less solvent.	
A higher quick ratio is a clear indicator of overtrading.	
The change in both the current and quick ratios could be explained by the increase in the receivables period.	

Working capital

The working capital cycle has worsened. This increases the possibility of Bonanza overtrading.	
There is a welcome improvement in the working capital cycle, mainly due to the change in the payment period for payables.	
The working capital cycle is worse than a year ago because of the change in inventory days.	

Overall performance

Despite overall growth, Bonanza is having a difficult year in 20X6 and needs to investigate why key ratios are deteriorating.	
20X6 looks to be a disaster for Bonanza.	
There is no evidence of possible control problems.	

32   BONANZA – COMPETITOR ANALYSIS

Chris Burke, the Finance Director, is preparing a presentation for the board of directors to discuss possible control problems within the business. He has asked you to complete a comparative 'score card' of key financial ratios comparing Bonanza and one of its main rivals, which he will use as part of his presentation.

Relevant data has been extracted for Bonanza as follows.

Extracts from accounts of Rival	Y/E 31/12/20X5
	£000
Profitability	
Sales revenue	10,000
Cost of sales	7,070
Profit from operations	950
Assets	
Non-current assets	3,559
Inventories	1,162
Trade receivables	1,233
Total	**5,954**
Equities and liabilities	
Equity	3,958
Non-current liabilities	792
Trade payables	581
Bank overdraft	423
Tax liabilities	200
Total	**5,954**

(a)   Complete the scorecard by calculating the missing ratios.   **(10 marks)**

Y/e 31/12/X5	Bonanza	Rival
Profitability		
Gross profit %	45.4%	
Operating profit %	4.1%	9.5%
Return on capital employed	12.7%	
Liquidity ratios		
Current ratio	2.9:1	
Acid test/Quick ratio	1.8:1	0.6:1

Y/e 31/12/X5	Bonanza	Rival
Working capital days		
Inventory holding period	85 days	60 days
Trade receivables collection period	67 days	45 days
Trade payables payment period	74 days	
Working capital cycle	78 days	

(b) **Assess the following statements concerning potential control problems and indicate whether they are true or false.** **(10 marks)**

Statement	True	False
The difference in gross margins could be explained by the Rival giving excessive sales discounts to shift excess inventory.		
Bonanza has delayed paying suppliers at the year end, which would contribute to the difference in current ratios.		
The difference in the lengths of the working capital cycles could be explained by a credit controller at Bonanza being off work due to illness.		
A warehouse employee in Bonanza was found to have stolen toy cars and sold them on an online auction site. This would contribute to the difference in the ROCE figures.		
Inadequate controls over expense claims for managers within Bonanza could contribute to the difference in the operating margins figures.		

33 CASH AND PROFIT

The directors of Bonanza have been having a discussion on the financial ratios of the business and which should take priority for the business.

Judith King (Managing Director) stated "All that seems to matter is profit and profit-based ratios. Every time I watch a business program on television, profit is pretty much the first thing that is talked about." It is for this reason that I have instructed the accounts department to delay the payment of our next rent bill. This should increase our profitability at a vital time as I am meeting the bank soon to discuss future funding.

Lech Polaski (Production Director) in part agreed but added "I feel that cash flow and liquidity ratios are also vital. However, at the end of the day cash and profit seem to be the same thing. I spend money on materials or wages and the same figure ends up in the profit and loss account, so if we are profitable we must have more cash coming in that going out."

Chris Burke (Finance Director) is a little despairing of his friends and colleagues and has asked you summarise the issue of 'profits versus cash' for him to use at the next board meeting where he will attempt to explain.

Briefly explain the profits and cash issues mentioned above under the following headings:

Why is profit important in business?	(5 marks)

Why must cash also be considered in business?	(5 marks)

Does the cash equal the profit?	(5 marks)

Discuss whether delaying the rent payment will be effective in increasing profits and the ethical stance the accounting department should take to the request.	(5 marks)

TASK 1.6

Assessment objective 6	Analyse the internal controls of an organisation and make recommendations.

34 BONANZA'S INVENTORY STOCK TAKE

You have been asked to review the arrangements for Bonanza's year-end inventory count to be undertaken at the central warehouse on 31 December 20X6, which happens this year to be a Saturday. This will be a working day, so there will continue to be movements of new games and toys in and out of the warehouse during the count. These will be kept to a minimum where possible.

The different categories of toys are stored within the first 20 aisles of the warehouse. Materials and components for the factory are stored in the last 10 aisles.

The following arrangements have been made for the inventory count:

The warehouse manager will supervise the count as he is most familiar with the inventory. There will be five teams of counters and each team will contain two members of staff, one from the finance department and another one volunteered from head office. None of the warehouse staff, other than the manager, will be involved in the count.

Each team will count an aisle of goods by counting up and then down each aisle. As this process is systematic, it is not felt that the team will need to flag areas once counted. Once the team has finished counting an aisle, they will hand in their sheets and be given a set for another aisle of the warehouse. In addition to the above, to assist with the inventory counting, there will be two teams of counters from the internal audit department and they will perform inventory counts.

The count sheets are sequentially numbered, and the product codes and descriptions are printed on them but no quantities. If the counters identify any inventory which is not on their sheets, then they are to enter the item on a separate sheet, which is not numbered. Once all counting is complete, the sequence of the sheets is checked and any additional sheets are also handed in at this stage. All sheets are completed in ink.

Sometimes the packaging on toys and games can be damaged to such an extent it is not possible for them to be sold except at a discount. Also, some materials and components can become obsolete as the toys concerned become replaced and outdated. Any damaged or obsolete items identified by the counters will be left where they are but the counter is to make a note on the inventory sheets detailing the level of damage.

For the inventory count arrangements of Bonanza identify and explain FIVE deficiencies; and provide a recommendation to address each deficiency.   **(15 marks)**

Deficiency	Recommendation

35   BONANZA'S SALES AND DESPATCH SYSTEM

As a result of poor customer feedback over service levels, Lech Polaski (Production Director) has started to investigate in detail where the problems are arising. He is reasonably happy over the way independent reatilers are dealing with customers but has concerns over telephone and website transactions.

Other than through stores, sales orders are mainly placed through Bonanza's website but some are also made via telephone.

Online orders are automatically checked against inventory records for availability; telephone orders, however, are checked manually by order clerks after the call. A follow-up call is usually made to customers if there is insufficient inventory. When taking telephone orders, clerks note down the details on plain paper and afterwards they complete a three part pre-printed order form. These order forms are not sequentially numbered and are sent manually to both despatch and the accounts department.

As the company is expanding, customers are able to place online orders which will exceed their agreed credit limit by 10%. Online orders are automatically forwarded to the despatch and accounts department.

A daily pick list is printed by the despatch department and this is used by the warehouse team to despatch goods. The goods are accompanied by a despatch note and all customers are required to sign a copy of this. On return, the signed despatch notes are given to the warehouse team to file.

The sales quantities are entered from the despatch notes and the authorised sales prices are generated by the invoicing system. If a discount has been given, say for supplying a used cartridge, then this has to be manually entered by the sales clerk onto the invoice.

Due to the expansion of the company, and as there is a large number of sale invoices, extra accounts staff have been asked to help out temporarily with producing the sales invoices. Normally it is only two sales clerks who produce the sales invoices.

Identify and explain FIVE deficiencies in Bonanza's sales and despatch system and provide a recommendation to address each of these deficiencies.   **(15 marks)**

Deficiency	Recommendation

Deficiency	Recommendation

36 BONANZA'S GENERAL LEDGER SYSTEM

Bonanza's general ledger is controlled by Chris Burke (Finance Director/FD) and Harry Archer (Chief Accountant or CA) with either of these people able to make independent journal entries. Chris and Harry are friends and keen skiers and do like to get away over the winter to take in the slopes. This isn't always easy to arrange as the year-end work needs to finish quickly to enable this holiday to take place. Tanisha Prince (Sales Director/SD) is given access to the general ledger over the skiing period in the unlikely event further adjustments are needed.

Chris does not require prior sight of the journals prepared by Harry as there is considerable trust between the two.

Anyone with general ledger access can create new general ledger accounts.

New slow moving inventory accounting policy

During the current year, the approach taken to accounting for slow moving inventory has been investigated by Harry. As customer taste changes then the level of inventory for toys needed also change and this can sometimes leave Bonanza with unsaleable items. When this happens, a provision is made to reflect the potential loss held within inventory. Harry has long felt that the existing approach was excessively prudent. The current approach is that when monthly sales of a line drop to below 50% of the previous year's monthly average, then all remaining inventory is written down to 50% of their value effectively writing off half the inventory held. Harry has decided to reduce the write-down to 10% of the inventory value.

This decision was taken by Harry just before his annual holiday and so he instructed Tanisha to make the appropriate adjustments.

Identify and explain five weaknesses in the general ledger system and suggest an improvement for each weakness to reduce the risk of error or misstatement. **(15 marks)**

Weakness	Suggestion for improvement

Weakness	Suggestion for improvement

Section 3

ANSWERS TO PRACTICE QUESTIONS

TASK 1.1

Assessment objective 1	Demonstrate an understanding of the roles and responsibilities of the accounting function within an organisation and examine ways of preventing and detecting fraud and systemic weaknesses.

1 STATUTORY DUTY

Who has the statutory duty to prepare accounts for BONANZA?

The company auditors.	
The directors of the company.	✓
Chris Burke, Finance Director.	
Harry Archer, Chief Accountant.	
Companies House.	

2 RESPONSIBILITY

Who is responsible for maintaining sound risk management and internal control systems within BONANZA?

The company auditors.	
The directors of the company.	✓
Chris Burke, Finance Director.	
Harry Archer, Chief Accountant.	
Companies House.	

3 BANK RECONCILIATION 1

Adjustment	Amount £	Debit/Credit
Adjustment for (2)	106	Cr
Adjustment for (3)	350	Dr
Adjustment for (4)	1,645	Dr

Note:

Reconciliation			
Cash book			
Balance b/d	103	ADJUSTMENT (2)	106
ADJUSTMENT (3)	350		
ADJUSTMENT (4)	1,645		
		Balance c/d	1,992
	2,098		2,098

Balance of bank account	363
Uncleared lodgements	1,629
	1,992

4 BANK RECONCILIATION 2

	Yes	No
A customer was accidentally invoiced twice for the same item.		✓
An independent retailer took a 2% prompt payment discount despite not having paid within the timescales required to earn a discount.		✓
Bank interest received had not been posted to the cash book.	✓	
A payment to a supplier of £2,500 had accidentally been posted as £250.	✓	

5 SALES LEDGER CONTROL ACCOUNT RECONCILIATION 1

	Add/Subtract	£
Total from list of balances		31,100
Adjustment for (a)	Add	65
Adjustment for (b)	Subtract	280
Adjustment for (c)	Subtract	1,170
Adjustment for (d)	Add	3,600
Adjustment for (e)	Subtract	99
Adjustment for (f)	Subtract	100
Revised total to agree with SLCA		33,116

6   SALES LEDGER CONTROL ACCOUNT RECONCILIATION 2

	Yes	No
A customer was accidentally invoiced twice for the same item.		✓
An independent retailer was sold items at the wrong price.		✓
Credit balances had been omitted from the list of receivables balances.	✓	
A payment from a customer of £230 had accidentally been posted as £320 to their individual account in the receivables ledger.	✓	

7   PURCHASES LEDGER CONTROL ACCOUNT RECONCILIATION

	Add/Subtract	£
Total from list of balances		132,589
Adjustment for (a)	Add	445
Adjustment for (b)	Subtract	4,340
Adjustment for (c)	Subtract	1,200
Adjustment for (d)	Subtract	132
Adjustment for (e)	Add	2,100
Adjustment for (f)	Add	120
Revised total to agree with PLCA		129,582

8   ERRORS

   (a)   **Journal**

	Dr £	Cr £
Motor expenses	4,500	
Motor vehicles at cost		4,500

   (b)   **Journal**

	Dr £	Cr £
Office sundries	16	
Suspense		16

(c)   **Journal**

	Dr £	Cr £
Closing inventory – statement of financial position	189,320	
Closing inventory – statement of profit or loss		189,320

Working

Inventory is valued at the lower of cost and net realisable value. The selling price is given as £227,184. To get to the selling price, 20% of the value of the cost is added to the cost. The cost of £189,320 has been calculated by dividing the selling price by 120 and then multiplying by 100. (227,184/120) × 100 = 189,320.

The value of closing inventory, in accordance with IAS 2 is £189,320.

(d)   **Journal**

	Dr £	Cr £
Receivables	1,720	
Discounts allowed		1,720
Discounts allowed	1,270	
Receivables		1,270

9   CHANGEOVER

Which TWO of the following controls can mitigate the risk of system failure during direct changeover?

Testing	✓
Training	
System documentation	
Data backup	✓
Check digits	

Note: Testing reduces the probability of failure, and data backup reduces the impact.

10 INFORMATION SYSTEM CONTROLS

	Security	Integrity
Locked doors	✓	
Passwords	✓	
Batch totals		✓
Reconciliation		✓
CCTV	✓	
Check digits		✓
Authorisation of data entry		✓
Fire alarms	✓	

11 PURCHASE CYCLE CONTROLS 1

Which TWO of the following controls in a purchase cycle could be implemented to reduce the risk of payment of goods not received?

Sequentially pre-numbered purchase requisitions and sequence check.	
Matching of goods received note with purchase invoice.	✓
Goods are inspected for condition and quantity and agreed to purchase order before acceptance.	✓
Daily update of inventory system.	

12 PURCHASE CYCLE CONTROLS 2

Which TWO of the following controls in the purchase cycle could be implemented to reduce the risk of procurement of unnecessary goods and services?

Centralised purchasing department.	✓
Sequentially pre-numbered purchase requisitions and sequence check.	
Orders can only be placed with suppliers from the approved suppliers list.	
All purchase requisitions are signed as authorised by an appropriate manager.	✓

13 EXPENSE CLAIM CONTROLS

Which ONE of the following essential internal control measures is evidently missing from Bonanza Ltd?

Bonanza lacks a control environment as the board are not setting an ethical tone at the top.	✓
Bonanza lacks an Internal Audit department.	
Bonanza lacks an experienced finance manager.	
Bonanza lacks an external auditor.	

14 PASSWORDS 1

Which of the following would be the most secure?

24june1963	
LaraJo	
mypassword	
Qwerty123!#	✓

15 PASSWORDS 2

Which TWO of the following would reduce the effectiveness of passwords?

Requirement that passwords are changed every two weeks	
Users are allowed to choose their own passwords	✓
Automatic lock-out after 3 failed attempts to access system	
Making the sharing of passwords a disciplinary offence	
Displaying the password on the screen when entered	✓

16 INTERNAL CONTROLS 1

Match each of the following activities to the component that it illustrates.

	Control environment	Information system	Control activities
The process of preparing the financial statements		✓	
Locking the inventory storeroom			✓

17 INTERNAL CONTROLS 2

Match each of the following activities to the type of control that it illustrates.

	Authorisation	Information processing	Physical control
The financial controller will count petty cash on a weekly basis			✓
There will be two keys to the locked safe: one held by the FD and the other by the MD.			✓

18   INTERNAL CONTROLS 3

Match each of the following activities to the type of computer control that it illustrates.

	General	Application
Storing extra copies of programs and data files off-site	✓	
New programmes to check data fields on input transactions		✓
Manual checks to ensure that input data were authorised		✓
Password protection limiting access to data	✓	
Range checks on payroll processing		✓
Manual checks to ensure that timesheets are authorised before details are processed		✓

19   INTERNAL CONTROLS 4

Indicate whether the following limitations are true or false.

	True	False
The cost of implementing controls may be more expensive than the benefits gained due to reduced risk	✓	
The effectiveness of many controls rely on the integrity of those applying them	✓	
Internal controls are only applied to material items		✓
Standard controls may not be designed to deal with unusual transactions	✓	

20   FRAUD 1

Which THREE of the following control activities would best prevent this fraud occurring?

Segregation of duties between cash handling and recording	✓
Post opening by two people	✓
Investigation of differences between website sales and cash banked	
Regular banking of cash and cheques received in the post	✓

21   FRAUD 2

Which ONE of the following control activities would best prevent this occurring?

Payroll standing data periodically printed out and checked on a line-by-line basis to independently held employee details	
Use of hierarchical passwords over standing data files	✓
Pre-authorisation of all amendments to payroll standing data by an independent official	
Supervision of the wages pay out by an independent official	

> **Note:** In order to prevent this from happening, the key is that fictitious employees never make it onto the payroll.
>
> - Printing out and checking standing data will detect any fictitious employees added but will not prevent them from being added.
>
> - Use of hierarchical passwords over standing data files ensures that an unscrupulous employee cannot access the part of the system where new employees would be added and hence will prevent the fraud. This is therefore the correct answer.
>
> - Pre-authorisation of all amendments will not prevent the addition as an unscrupulous employee will not ask for authorisation but will simply add the fictitious details if the system allows them to do this.
>
> - Supervision of the wages pay out by an independent official might detect dummy employees but would be unlikely to prevent the fraud.

TASK 1.2

Assessment objective 2	Evaluate budgetary reporting; its effectiveness in controlling and improving organisational performance.

22 TRAINING COSTS

(a) **BRIEFLY discuss THREE weaknesses in the above use of performance reports to improve the focus of training within BONANZA.**

Weakness 1
Flexing
The budget is a fixed one; meaning it has not been flexed for the 25% increase in activity.
A flexible budget is one where the turnover and variable costs are changed in line with the change in activity. In this case they would be increased by 25%. Fixed costs remain unchanged from the original budget.
The advantage of fixed budgeting is that it takes less time and is, therefore, less costly to produce; the disadvantage is that variances are less meaningful and, therefore, control is effectively reduced. The advantage and disadvantage of flexible budgeting are the opposite of this.
The flexed budget cost would be
$$13,000 + 1,000 \times (25/20) = £14,250$$
This gives an overall favourable variance of £150 rather than an adverse one of £100. The manager should thus be praised rather than reprimanded.
Weakness 2
Participation in target setting and budgeting
Petr Higgs was not involved in setting the original budget and did not even know about it. This lack of participation could easily result in him viewing the target as unfair and unrealistic, resulting in demotivation. It is also very difficult to be motivated to hit a target you are unaware of!

Greater participation will help resolve these issues and also may result in more realistic budgets in the first place. The main disadvantage of participation is the possibility of budget "padding", where Petr may have tried to set an easy target for himself.

Weakness 3

Emphasis on financial factors

The sole emphasis on financial factors only may result in Petr being more concerned about cost control than delivering high quality training.

The directors were concerned that training lacked focus rather than it being too expensive. There is nothing in the email to see if focus has improved.

Weakness 4

Lech Polaski's tone

Lech Polaski's tone is far too aggressive, particularly given the above factors, and is likely to result in resentment and demotivation.

This is particularly the case as it is the first month of the new system, so there is a significant possibility that budgeted figures are not representative in the first place. The variance could thus be due to planning errors rather than Petr's operational performance.

(b)   Outline THREE performance indicators that could be used to assess the quality of the training provided.

Performance Indicator 1

Trainee feedback

Trainees could be asked to score different elements of the training process on a score of 1 to 5 say. This would indicate whether or not they felt the training was useful to them and would indicate areas for improvement.

Performance Indicator 2

Manager feedback

Presumably managers had objectives when sending staff on training courses/events – for example, to improve IT skills. Managers could be asked to assess whether they felt that their staff had benefited from the training – for example, were they more able to undertake required tasks in their roles? Again, a score of 1 to 5 would allow easier monitoring of feedback.

Performance Indicator 3

Objective scoring using tests

For some training – for example, awareness of company products – it may be possible to set a quiz or test before and after training to see if trainee's knowledge and awareness had improved.

(Total 15 marks)

23   BUDGETING

Evaluate the Bonanza budget for 20X6 by reference to the following assumed (or implied) growth rates and margins. In your answer discuss whether or not you feel the figures are realistic and why.
(15 marks)

Figure	Whether or not realistic
Sales volume growth of 10.0%	Growth of 10% seems very optimistic, especially given the downturn in the global macro-economic environment and the threat from substitute products such as video games. These have resulted in industry forecast growth of only 5.0%.
	However, Bonanza is planning to release five new games and has received a boost to its reputation by winning an industry award at the end of 20X5.
Sales revenue growth of 8.0%	Compared to volume growth of 10%, sales growth of 8% seems more reasonable.
	The difference would imply a fall in the average price, either due to a cut in prices or a change is sales mix.
	Either of these factors could be explained by increased competition or a decision to cut average prices to deal with competition from video games.
Cost of sales growth of 7.0%	Cost of sales growth of only 7% seems low compared to sales volume growth of 10%.
	One way of explaining this difference between would only be feasible if a significant proportion of cost of sales were fixed costs rather than variable. This seems unlikely as the main part of cost of sales will be price of games from the Indian supplier.
	Alternatively it may be that the sales manager is incorporating the strengthening GBP in estimates as this will reduce the effective cost of paying Indian Rupees to the supplier.
Gross margin of 48.7%	If the above assumptions regarding growth hold to be valid, then the end result will be a gpm of 48.7%.
	Furthermore, the increase is only small compared to the actual figures achieved in 20X5.
Fall in selling costs of 1.3%	A significant proportion of selling and distribution costs can be expected to be variable, so it is questionable how Bonanza expects to see these costs fall by 1.3% when sales volume is increasing by 10%.
	As stated above, the only way this could happen would be if a significant amount of costs were designated in foreign currencies and so Bonanza would benefit from the movement in exchange rates.

Fall in administration costs of 17.5%	Administration costs are likely to be mainly fixed in nature, so the only way such a large decrease can be achieved would be as a result of significant cost efficiencies.
	There is no information to suggest that such cost savings are feasible.

Conclusion – whether or not the budget is realistic

Overall the budget looks over-optimistic. In particular it is difficult to justify the change in cost of sales and the fall in selling and admin costs.

24 BONANZA BUDGETING PROCESS

Strengths

- Inflation should be allowed for as this leads to more accurate budgets

- Materials costs seem to be accounted for correctly

- Marketing seems to be based on only those products that the directors wish to specifically promote, reducing the possibility of cost overspends or unfocussed marketing expenditure

- Some attempt is made to account for the effectiveness of the marketing spend using regression analysis

Weaknesses

- Whilst choice over RPI and CPI is good for motivation it can lead to inconsistency and confusion for managers that are unaware of the difference and appropriateness of these.

- No inflationary guidance is given for costs other than wages, rents and materials implying that these other costs are "minor". This therefore excludes, for example, the cost of games made in India, which is far from minor. Equally many minor costs can add up to a lot and hence a large potential error

- Past inflation is not necessarily equal to future inflation - for example, after the Brexit vote in the UK, inflation jumped considerably compared to past measures

- Rent might not be affected by inflation at all. Leases have fixed rent review points and can sometimes be influenced by general market condition as well as inflation

- Other sales managers are not consulted on any local marketing need. This can be demotivating and might not address concerns over poor performance – for example, Jenni Black may feel that Bonanza needs to spend more promoting its online presence

- Past marketing to sales trends may not continue given the ever-changing markets

- Sales volumes change for other reasons (not just marketing)

Opportunities

- A central decision should be made regarding the inflation measure to be used

- More complete inflationary guidance could be given to include all costs lines

- Guidance could be given concerning rental budgets, suggesting that existing leases be reviewed for rent revision dates

- Greater account could be given to current market conditions when predicting sales (rather than relying purely on past regression)

Threats

- If inflation is under estimated on a cost then this could lead to an under budgeted costs and adverse variances. The opposite is true for overestimated inflation

- Omission of inflationary guidance for (in particular) cost of sales could lead to a significant budget error, loss of confidence in the process and under funding

- Sales levels may disappoint if no local considerations are made

- Assuming that the past will continue into the future is misguided and new opportunities may be missed or complacency could set in

- Budget sales levels could be incorrect leading to poor assumptions about profitability

TASK 1.3

Assessment objective 3	Evaluate an organisation's accounting control systems and procedures.

25 BONANZA'S PURCHASING SYSTEM

Required:

Identify and explain FOUR deficiencies in the system, explain the possible implication of each deficiency and provide a recommendation to address each deficiency. **(15 marks)**

Deficiency	Implication	Recommendation
When raising purchase orders, the clerks choose whichever supplier can dispatch the goods the fastest.	This could result in Bonanza ordering goods at a much higher price or a lower quality than they would like, as the only factor considered was speed of delivery. It is important that goods are dispatched promptly, but this is just one of many criteria that should be used in deciding which supplier to use.	An approved supplier list should be compiled; this should take into account the price of goods, their quality and also the speed of delivery. Once the list has been produced, all orders should only be placed with suppliers on the approved list.

Purchase orders are not sequentially numbered.	Failing to sequentially number the orders means that Bonanza's ordering team is unable to monitor if all orders are being fulfilled in a timely manner; this could result in stock outs. If the orders are numbered, then a sequence check can be performed for any unfulfilled orders.	All purchase orders should be sequentially numbered and on a regular basis a sequence check of unfulfilled orders should be performed.
Purchase orders below £1,000 are not authorised and are processed solely by an order clerk.	This can result in goods being purchased which are not required by Bonanza. In addition, there is an increased fraud risk as an order clerk could place orders for personal goods up to the value of £1,000, which is significant.	All purchase orders should be authorised by a responsible official. Authorised signatories should be established with varying levels of purchase order authorisation.
Purchase invoices are input daily by the purchase ledger clerk and due to his experience, he does not utilise any application controls.	Without application controls there is a risk that invoices could be input into the system with inaccuracies or they may be missed out entirely. This could result in suppliers being paid incorrectly or not all, leading to a loss of supplier goodwill.	The purchase ledger clerk should input the invoices in batches and apply application controls, such as control totals, to ensure completeness and accuracy over the input of purchase invoices.
The purchase day book automatically updates with the purchase ledger but this ledger is manually posted to the general ledger.	Manually posting the amounts to the general ledger increases the risk of errors occurring. This could result in the payables balance in the financial statements being under or overstated.	The process should be updated so that on a regular basis the purchase ledger automatically updates the general ledger. A responsible official should then confirm through purchase ledger control account reconciliations that the update has occurred correctly.

Bonanza's saving (deposit) bank accounts are only reconciled every two months.	If these accounts are only reconciled periodically, there is the risk that errors will not be spotted promptly. Also, this increases the risk of employees committing fraud. If they are aware that these accounts are not regularly reviewed, then they could use these cash sums fraudulently.	All bank accounts should be reconciled on a regular basis, and at least monthly, to identify any unusual or missing items. The reconciliations should be reviewed by a responsible official and they should evidence their review.
Bonanza has a policy of delaying payments to their suppliers for as long as possible.	Whilst this maximises Bonanza's bank balance, there is the risk that Bonanza is missing out on early settlement discounts. Also, this can lead to a loss of supplier goodwill as well as the risk that suppliers may refuse to supply goods to Bonanza.	Bonanza should undertake cash flow forecasting/ budgeting to maximise bank balances. The policy of delaying payment should be reviewed, and suppliers should be paid in a systematic way, such that supplier goodwill is not lost.

Note: only FOUR required.

26 BONANZA'S SALES AND INVENTORY PROCESSES

Required:

In respect of the internal control of Bonanza's sales and inventory processes, identify FIVE deficiencies, explain the possible implication of each deficiency and recommend a control to address each of these deficiencies. **(15 marks)**

Deficiency	Implication	Recommendation
Currently the website is not integrated into inventory system.	This can result in Bonanza accepting customer orders when they do not have the goods in inventory. This can cause them to lose sales and customer goodwill.	The website should be updated to include an interface into the inventory system; this should check inventory levels and only process orders if adequate inventory is held. If inventory is out of stock, this should appear on the website with an approximate waiting time.

For goods despatched by local couriers, customer signatures are not always obtained.	This can lead to customers falsely claiming that they have not received their goods. Bonanza would not be able to prove that they had in fact despatched the goods and may result in goods being despatched twice.	Bonanza should remind all local couriers that customer signatures must be obtained as proof of despatch and payment will not be made for any despatches with missing signatures.
There have been a number of situations where the sales orders have not been fulfilled in a timely manner.	This can lead to a loss of customer goodwill and if it persists will damage the reputation of Bonanza as a reliable supplier.	Once goods are despatched they should be matched to sales orders and flagged as fulfilled. The system should automatically flag any outstanding sales orders past a predetermined period, such as five days. This report should be reviewed by a responsible official.
Customer credit limits are set by sales ledger clerks.	Sales ledger clerks are not sufficiently senior and so may set limits too high, leading to irrecoverable debts, or too low, leading to a loss of sales.	Credit limits should be set by a senior member of the sales ledger department and not by sales ledger clerks. These limits should be regularly reviewed by a responsible official.
Sales discounts are set by Bonanza's sales team.	In order to boost their sales, members of the sales team may set the discounts too high, leading to a loss of revenue.	All members of the sales team should be given authority to grant sales discounts up to a set limit. Any sales discounts above these limits should be authorised by sales area managers or the sales director. Regular review of sales discount levels should be undertaken by the sales director, and this review should be evidenced.

Supplier statement reconciliations are no longer performed.	This may result in errors in the recording of purchases and payables not being identified in a timely manner.	Supplier statement reconciliations should be performed on a monthly basis for all suppliers and these should be reviewed by a responsible official.
Changes to supplier details in the purchase ledger master file can be undertaken by purchase ledger clerks.	This could lead to key supplier data being accidently amended or fictitious suppliers being set up, which can increase the risk of fraud.	Only purchase ledger supervisors should have the authority to make changes to master file data. This should be controlled via passwords. Regular review of any changes to master file data by a responsible official and this review should be evidenced.
Bonanza has considerable levels of surplus plant and equipment.	Surplus unused plant is at risk of theft. In addition, if the surplus plant is not disposed of then the company could lose sundry income.	Regular review of the plant and equipment on the factory floor by senior factory personnel to identify any old or surplus equipment. As part of the capital expenditure process there should be a requirement to confirm the treatment of the equipment being replaced.
Purchase requisitions are authorised by production supervisors.	Production supervisors are not sufficiently independent or senior to authorise capital expenditure.	Capital expenditure authorisation levels to be established. Production supervisors should only be able to authorise low value items, any high value items should be authorised by the board.

Note: only FIVE required.

27   BONANZA'S INVENTORY COUNTING PROCESSES

Weakness	Effect of Weakness
The internal auditor should attend as an observer only and not get involved in the count itself. To do so confuses the roles of the people involved.	Errors in process might not have been detected as the internal auditor was busy "doing" rather than "observing". It is also possible that the internal auditor who is not an employee is not competent to recognize damaged or slow moving inventory and so these items could go unrecorded.
Weakness	**Effect of Weakness**
The instructions are capable of misinterpretation. Staff seem to have been instructed to record all items that are shown on the sheets as being in a certain location. They might not record items that are therefore in the wrong location, or only look in designated locations rather than all possible places where inventory may be held.	This could lead to serious understatement of the inventory values and hence an understatement of profit.
The designation of duties is a little unclear. The two unallocated zones appear to fall between two counting teams and so the count is then dependent on the organisation of the spare resource on the count day.	An area could either be missed or be counted by both teams. This could lead to over or under statement of the inventory and hence profit.
The delivery that took place on the day of the count might not have been accounted for properly. It is not clear from the question what happened to the actual counting of the delivery. The items should have been included, even though they were in the car park at the time. Equally, details of the delivery should have been recorded so that correct cut off with regards to purchases could subsequently be checked.	The items could have been incorrectly excluded and so inventory understated. Without delivery details being recorded a cut off error could have occurred. Consistency between the recording of inventory and the recording of purchases is important and without this the incorrect profit will be calculated.
Box labelling was relied on for the contents of boxes. This is an unreliable method. Damaged items within the boxes would not be identified.	Inventory could be misstated as the content of the boxes might not reflect the labelling. If damaged items are not identified then the inventory will be overstated.
Old items (slow-moving) were not identified or recorded during the count.	The accounting policy cannot be checked against the actual figures and so Bonanza might not detect and error in that policy.

Note: only FIVE required.

TASK 1.4

Assessment objective 4	Analyse an organisation's decision making and control using management accounting tools.

28 PRODUCTION DECISIONS

(a) BRIEFLY discuss the validity of each of the three directors' views on how the final decision should be made as to which cars to make. **(9 marks)**

Managing Director
The Managing Director is basing decisions on the reported profits of each product. The reported operating profits include an arbitrary allocation of fixed costs that undermines their credibility.
While the Managing Director is correct that fixed costs must be covered somewhere, they are irrelevant to the decision as they are by definition unavoidable regardless of the decision.
Decisions should be made on the basis of future incremental cash flows.
Sales Director
The Sales Director is basing decisions on the contribution of each product. This has the advantage of considering only the future relevant cash flows and ignoring the allocated fixed overheads.
Looking at total contribution would only be appropriate if there was enough space to stock sufficient toys to meet full demand, which is not the case here.
Unit contribution would be appropriate if all toys involved the same amount of skilled labour, but, again, this is not the case here.
Production Director
The Production Director has the best overall approach as he is considering contribution, thus looking at relevant cash flows and ignoring allocated overheads.
In addition, and unlike the Sales Director, he is then incorporating how much time is taken to make each car. The ranking based on contribution per unit of scarce resource (i.e. time) should ensure that the use of skilled labour is maximised to generate the most contribution possible.

(b) BRIEFLY explain THREE other factors should be taken into consideration before making a final decision. **(6 marks)**

Factor 1
How much labour is available
The decision is focussed on selecting just one car to stock. However, it may be that there is sufficient labour to make many ranges, even if there is not enough for all of them.
For example, making 4,000 Ds would need $4,000 \times 11 = 44,000$ minutes. This is sufficient for all of the Cs (requires $2,000 \times 12 = 24,000$) and a significant number of Bs, say.
Furthermore, it may be possible to increase the amount of available labour by asking staff to work overtime, although the overtime premium paid would have to be factored into the contribution calculations.

Factor 2
Whether customers are willing to wait
For some older cars, customers may be happy to order on the website and wait until the next production run of those models. If this is the case, then Bonanza could simply wait until they have a month with spare capacity and make these models then

Factor 3
The figures used
The decision has been based on the figures available. However, these may change, possibly affecting the decision.
For example, discounts have been ignored but if one car tends to attract more discounts, say to boost falling demand, then the price (and hence contribution per minute) would fall, changing the ranking.

29 NEW SUPPLIERS

(a) **Which of the following prices should be used for target costing?** (2 marks)

The budgeted price that Bonanza has set for 20X6	✓
The existing price that Bonanza uses	
The market average price	
The price charged by Bonanza's main competitor for a similar game	

(b) **Calculate the target cost for the AX159 toy.** (3 marks)

Cost per unit	£
Production cost (charged by supplier)	15.50
Transportation costs (given)	2.50
Total cost = 25.20 × (100/140)	**18.00**
Mark up = 25.20 × 40/140	7.20
Target selling price	**25.20**

(c) **Briefly explain how the concept of value analysis applies to Bonanza and the options available to it to close any cost gap.** (4 marks)

Value analysis
Value analysis involves considering which aspects of the product are valued by the customer.
This would allow Bonanza to identify possible areas for cutting costs to close any target cost 'gap' without compromising the value to the customer.
For Bonanza the ultimate consumer will value the playability of the games, so aspects such as the game's rules, complexity and so on should not be compromised.
However, customers may be less concerned about the quality of packaging or the materials used for the character pieces.

Options available to Bonanza
Bonanza may be able to reduce transportation costs by choosing suppliers who are closer.
Apart from this the only option is to get lower prices from suppliers, whether through cheaper materials or switching suppliers.
Obviously it must be careful not to compromise customer perceived quality when doing this.

(d) **Discuss which supplier should be chosen by referring to both financial and non-financial factors.**
                                                                                    (6 marks)

Financial factors
Target cost
Both suppliers B and C meet the target cost criteria, with C being the cheapest.
However, A may meet the target cost depending on the extent of any bulk discount offered.
This may be significant as the "Escape from the Island" is Bonanza's most popular game.
Non-financial factors
Quality of supply
The main problem with C is the long delivery time as this will either mean potential delays to customers or that mean that Bonanza will need to hold higher inventory levels. Delays to customers should be avoided given the downturn in customer loyalty and satisfaction. On the other hand, holding more inventory will increase the length of the cash operating cycle. This may not be acceptable given recent cash flow problems. Delivery times would favour A and B.
Linked to cash flow problems we can also look at credit terms. Longer credit terms take the pressure off Bonanza's cash cycle suggesting that B should be chosen
Quality of product
It is important that customers feel that they are buying a quality product that reflects the brand.
Supplier C's board and character pieces may be seen as inferior to the current offering, so could erode brand perception and loyalty, especially if this gets discussed on social media.
Supplier B seems to be matching the current product, whereas Supplier A is improving quality by using metal pieces. Unfortunately this may mean that the cost is too high resulting in Bonanza failing to hit the required. It is also debatable whether customers would value metal pieces over polished wood.

30   BONANZA TOY TRAIN PLANNING

(a)   Data table:

Quarter Number	Volume Units	Revenue £	Variable Cost £	Contribution £
1 (Q1 2017)	1,430	71,500	42,900	28,600
2 (Q2 2017)	1,390	69,500	41,700	27,800
3 (Q3 2017)	1,330	66,500	39,900	26,600
4 (Q4 2017)	1,290	64,500	38,700	25,800
5 (Q1 2018)	1,230	61,500	36,900	24,600
6 (Q2 2018)	1,190	59,500	35,700	23,800
7 (Q3 2018)	1,140	57,000	34,200	22,800
8 (Q4 2018)	1,090	54,500	32,700	21,800
9 (Q1 2019)	1,040	52,000	31,200	20,800
10 (Q2 2019)	990	49,500	29,700	19,800

(b)   Discussion of findings:

> **The value 'b'**
>
> The value b is the slope of the regression line, indicating by how much the value y declines (in this case) and the x value increases by 1 (1 quarter in this case). Hence it shows the decline in sales volume as time ticks by one quarter at a time. This is based on past declines and there is no guarantee that past trend reflects the future. The decline could be greater or lower than the 50 units given.
>
> **Data findings**
>
> The data shows that this product's revenue will fall to £49,500 by the end of the planning horizon (Q2 2019). Over the same period the contribution gained also gradually falls and reaches only £19,800 by that same point.
>
> The important point is that Bonanza will continue to make a positive contribution up to that quarter and so should be willing to continue to supply the product.
>
> The data also states that this product's share of fixed costs are £20,000 and this might imply to some that cessation of supply is justified. However, it must be borne in mind that these fixed costs are not avoidable on cessation and as such are not relevant to a cessation decision.
>
> Furthermore, the data only relates to sales on engines of that range and does not include sales of matching carriages and other linked products

(c)   **Non-financial considerations**

> Businesses should not make all decisions purely based on the financial figures and this case is no different. The following considerations are worthy of note:
>
> Reaction of customers – customers that own other products in that particular range may feel abandoned if they can no longer source new engines. This could breed bad will at a time when customer goodwill has taken a downturn.
>
> Reaction of staff – some staff may specialise in making the particular range concerned and so may face either redundancy or the need to retrain if the range is discontinued.

TASK 1.5

Assessment objective 5	Analyse an organisation's decision making and control using ratio analysis.

31   BONANZA AND OVERTRADING

(a)   **Complete the scorecard by calculating the missing ratios.**   **(10 marks)**

BONANZA Scorecard	Y/e 31/12/X6	Y/e 31/12/X5
Profitability and gearing		
Gross profit %	38.4%	45.4%
Operating profit %	3.6%	4.1%
Return on capital employed	11.5%	12.7%
Gearing (debt/equity)	0.20×	0.12×
Liquidity ratios		
Current ratio	3.8:1	2.9:1
Acid test/Quick ratio	2.4:1	1.8:1
Working capital days		
Inventory holding period	70 days	85 days
Trade receivables collection period	71 days	67 days
Trade payables payment period	60 days	74 days
Working capital cycle	81 days	78 days

Workings

- Operating profit margin = (2,570/62,000) × 100% = 4.1%

- ROCE = 2,570/(18,137 + 2,168) × 100% = 12.7%

- Quick ratio = (20,851 – 7,916)/7,264 = 1.8×

- Inventory days = (7,916/33,864) × 365 = 85 days

- Working capital cycle = 85 + 67 – 74 = 78 days

(b) **Select the ONE correct observation about each aspect of business performance below.** **(10 marks)**

Profitability

20X6 will be a year of steady, if unspectacular, progress. Although margins have dipped, the return on capital employed has been kept constant.	
The changes in gross margin could be due to cost control problems concerning distribution.	
Increased competition and the resulting pressure on prices could explain the change in each of the three profitability ratios.	✓

Gearing

The increased gearing ratio proves that BONANZA has no problems raising additional debt finance.	
It is likely that the interest cover ratio has increased.	
The increased gearing ratio shows that the shareholders' position has become more risky.	✓

Liquidity

Both ratios have increased, which indicates that the company is less solvent.	
A higher quick ratio is a clear indicator of overtrading.	
The change in both the current and quick ratios could be explained by the increase in the receivables period.	✓

Working capital

The working capital cycle has worsened. This increases the possibility of BONANZA overtrading.	✓
There is a welcome improvement in the working capital cycle, mainly due to the change in the payment period for payables.	
The working capital cycle is worse than a year ago because of the change in inventory days.	

Overall performance

Despite overall growth, BONANZA is having a difficult year in 20X6 and needs to investigate why key ratios are deteriorating.	✓
20X6 looks to be a disaster for BONANZA.	
There is no evidence of possible control problems.	

32   BONANZA – COMPETITOR ANALYSIS

(a)   Complete the scorecard by calculating the missing ratios.   (10 marks)

Y/e 31/12/X5	Bonanza	Rival
Profitability		
Gross profit %	45.4%	**29.3%**
Operating profit %	4.1%	9.5%
Return on capital employed	12.7%	**20.0%**
Liquidity ratios		
Current ratio	2.9:1	**2.0:1**
Acid test/Quick ratio	1.8:1	0.6:1
Working capital days		
Inventory holding period	85 days	60 days
Trade receivables collection period	67 days	45 days
Trade payables payment period	74 days	**30 days**
Working capital cycle	78 days	**75 days**

(b)   Assess the following statements concerning potential control problems and indicate whether they are true or false.   (10 marks)

Statement	True	False
The difference in gross margins could be explained by the Rival giving excessive sales discounts to shift excess inventory.	✓	
Bonanza has delayed paying suppliers at the year end, which would contribute to the difference in current ratios.		✓
The difference in the lengths of the working capital cycles could be explained by a credit controller at Bonanza being off work due to illness.	✓	
A warehouse employee in Bonanza was found to have stolen toy cars and sold them on an online auction site. This would contribute to the difference in the ROCE figures.	✓	
Inadequate controls over expense claims for managers within Bonanza could contribute to the difference in the operating margins figures.	✓	

33   CASH AND PROFIT

Why is profit important in business? (5 marks)

Profits are the generally accepted measure of the successful trading of a business.

Profit is the most commonly used measure of performance with analysts looking at figures for profit, profit margins and return on capital employed. As such the determination of profit is heavily regulated.

This regulation (in the form of standard accounting practices) ensures that all companies measure profit is broadly the same way and in this way, it is trusted by investors and management to reflect performance.

The press often focusses on profitability when commenting on a business's performance and this tends to increase the profile of the profit measure on all concerned.

Why must cash also be considered in business? (5 marks)

Cash in this context is the cash balance of the business at any one time and also the amount of cash the business has generated or spent over the accounting period.

Cash is seen as vital in business for a number of reasons:

Cash is used for investment. If a business wants to buy assets in order to grow, then it needs cash to do that. It can borrow that money, that is true, but in this case it will need cash to make the repayments on any loan it takes out.

Cash is also used to make normal commercial payments. Wages, suppliers, and stationery, all must be paid for with cash and so without cash these payments cannot be made and trade would stop.

The government also have a stake in businesses and although the regulation insists that profits are measured the government requires that corporate tax is paid. Although the amount of tax is in part determined by the profits made the company needs cash to actually make the payment.

Cash might also be needed for emergencies, to cover for example unexpected payments. Businesses often hold reserves of cash for this purpose.

Does the cash equal the profit? (5 marks)

In some ways, what Lech says is true. If he buys materials from a supplier then that will have to be paid for with cash. However, one important difference here is the timing of the purchase compared to the payment. There is often a lag between the purchase and the subsequent payment. Consequently although the two figures are the same they will be recorded at different points of time.

Also, there are other cash transactions that are not reflected in the profits of the business immediately. For example, when a business buys a piece of plant the cash outflow would be immediate and in total. The expense in the profit and loss account would slowly catch up over a number of years as depreciation is charged over the assets useful economic life but there would be a significant delay in the case of long existing assets.

The final major difference created between cash and profits is dividend. Dividend is a cash outflow but does not go through the profit and loss account at all.

For all the above reasons the amount a business has in cash is not equal to the profitability of the same business. In extreme cases, companies can be guilty of 'over-trading' – trying to grow too quickly and run out of cash despite being profitable.

Discuss whether delaying the rent payment will be effective in increasing profits and the ethical stance the accounting department should take to the request. (5 marks)

The accounts of a business are produced using generally accepted accounting principles. One of these is matching. The principle is that over an accounting period expense are related to that period regardless of the cash transactions.

What this means is that if a rent payment is delayed (as is being suggested in this case) then it would still be necessary to reflect the full rent cost in the profit and loss account and an accrual entry would be made to record it.

Consequently, delaying the rent payment would not be effective in increasing profits.

Ethically the account staff will be bound by an ethical code and would therefore be expected to behave professionally and with due care. Where it is being suggested that an accounting error be deliberately made in order to manipulate the accounts then the accountants would have to resist and in some way refuse to make the adjustment.

TASK 1.6

Assessment objective 6	Analyse the internal controls of an organisation and make recommendations.

34 BONANZA'S INVENTORY STOCK TAKE

For the inventory count arrangements of Bonanza identify and explain FIVE deficiencies; and provide a recommendation to address each deficiency. (15 marks)

Deficiency	Recommendation
The warehouse manager is planning to supervise the inventory count. Whilst he is familiar with the inventory, he has overall responsibility for the inventory and so is not independent. He may want to hide inefficiencies and any issues that arise so that his department is not criticised.	An alternative supervisor who is not normally involved with the inventory, such as an internal audit manager, should supervise the inventory count. The warehouse manager and his team should not be involved in the count at all.
There are five teams of counters, each team having two members of staff. However, there is no clear division of responsibilities within the team. Therefore, both members of staff could count together rather than checking each other's count; and errors in their count may not be identified.	Each team should be informed that both members are required to count their assigned inventory separately. Therefore, one counts and the second member checks that the inventory has been counted correctly.
The internal audit teams are undertaking inventory counts rather than reviewing the controls and performing sample test counts. Their role should be focused on confirming the accuracy of the inventory counting procedures.	The internal audit counters should sample check the counting undertaken by the ten teams to provide an extra control over the completeness and accuracy of the count.

Deficiency	Recommendation
Once areas are counted, the teams are not flagging the aisles as completed. Therefore there is the risk that some areas of the warehouse could be double counted or missed out.	All aisles should be flagged as completed, once the inventory has been counted. In addition, internal audit or the count supervisor should check at the end of the count that all 20 aisles have been flagged as completed.
Inventory not listed on the sheets is to be entered onto separate sheets, which are not sequentially numbered. Therefore the supervisor will be unable to ensure the completeness of all inventory sheets.	Each team should be given a blank sheet for entering any inventory count which is not on their sheets. This blank sheet should be sequentially numbered, any unused sheets should be returned at the end of the count, and the supervisor should check the sequence of all sheets at the end of the count.
The sheets are completed in ink and are sequentially numbered, however, there is no indication that they are signed by the counting team. Therefore if any issues arise with the counting in an aisle, it will be difficult to follow up as the identity of the counting team will not be known.	All inventory sheets should be signed by the relevant team upon completion of an aisle. When the sheets are returned, the supervisor should check that they have been signed.
Damaged or obsolete toys and materials are not being stored in a central area, and instead the counter is just noting on the inventory sheets the level of damage or indicating obsolescence. However, it will be difficult for the finance team to decide on an appropriate level of write down if they are not able to see the damaged goods. In addition, if these goods are left in the aisles, they could be inadvertently sold to customers or moved to another aisle.	Damaged goods should be clearly flagged by the counting teams and moved to a central location. This will avoid the risk of selling these goods. A senior member of the finance team should then inspect these goods to assess the level of any write down or allowance.
The 31 December is a working day, so there will be movements of goods during the count. Inventory records could be under/overstated if goods are missed or double counted due to movements in the warehouse.	It may not be practical to stop all inventory movements as the business needs to continue. Any goods received from suppliers should be stored in one location and counted once at the end and included as part of raw materials. Goods to be despatched to customers should be kept to a minimum for the day of the count. It may make more sense to do the inventory check the next day on a Sunday.

Note: only FIVE required

35 BONANZA'S SALES AND DESPATCH SYSTEM

Identify and explain FIVE deficiencies in BONANZA's sales and despatch system and provide a recommendation to address each of these deficiencies. **(15 marks)**

Deficiency	Recommendation
Inventory availability for telephone orders is not checked at the time the order is placed. The order clerks manually check the availability later and only then inform customers if there is insufficient inventory available. There is the risk that where goods are not available, order clerks could forget to contact the customers, leading to unfulfilled orders. This could lead to customer dissatisfaction, and would impact BONANZA's reputation.	When telephone orders are placed, the order clerk should check the inventory system whilst the customer is on the phone; they can then give an accurate assessment of the availability of goods and there is no risk of forgetting to inform customers.
Telephone orders are not recorded immediately on the three part pre-printed order forms; these are completed after the telephone call. There is a risk that incorrect or insufficient details may be recorded by the clerk and this could result in incorrect orders being despatched or orders failing to be despatched at all, resulting in a loss of customer goodwill.	All telephone orders should be recorded immediately on the three part pre-printed order forms. The clerk should also double check all the details taken with the customer over the telephone to ensure the accuracy of the order recorded.
Telephone orders are not sequentially numbered. Therefore if orders are misplaced whilst in transit to the despatch department, these orders will not be fulfilled, resulting in dissatisfied customers.	The three part pre-printed orders forms should be sequentially numbered and on a regular basis the despatch department should run a sequence check of orders received. Where there are gaps in the sequence, they should be investigated to identify any missing orders.
Customers are able to place online orders which will exceed their agreed credit limit by 10%. This increases the risk of accepting orders from bad credit risks.	Customer credit limits should be reviewed more regularly by a responsible official and should reflect the current spending pattern of customers. If some customers have increased the level of their purchases and are making payments on time, then these customers' credit limits could be increased. The online ordering system should be amended to not allow any orders to be processed which will exceed the customer's credit limit.

Deficiency	Recommendation
A daily pick list is used by the despatch department when sending out customer orders. However, it does not appear that the goods are checked back to the original order; this could result in incorrect goods being sent out.	In addition to the pick list, copies of all the related orders should be printed on a daily basis. When the goods have been picked ready to be despatched, they should be cross checked back to the original order. They should check correct quantities and product descriptions, as well as checking the quality of goods being despatched to ensure they are not damaged.
Additional staff have been drafted in to help the two sales clerks produce the sales invoices. As the extra staff will not be as experienced as the sales clerks, there is an increased risk of mistakes being made in the sales invoices. This could result in customers being under or overcharged.	Only the sales clerks should be able to raise sales invoices. As BONANZA is expanding, consideration should be given to recruiting and training more permanent sales clerks who can produce sales invoices.
Discounts given to customers are manually entered onto the sales invoices by sales clerks. This could result in unauthorised sales discounts being given as there does not seem to be any authorisation required. In addition, a clerk could forget to manually enter the discount or enter an incorrect level of discount for a customer, leading to the sales invoice being overstated and a loss of customer goodwill.	For customers who are due to receive a discount, the authorised discount levels should be updated to the customer master file. When the sales invoices for these customers are raised, their discounts should automatically appear on the invoice. The invoicing system should be amended to prevent sales clerks from being able to manually enter sales discounts onto invoices.

Note: only FIVE required

36   BONANZA'S GENERAL LEDGER SYSTEM

Weakness	Suggestion for improvement
There appears to be no approval required for any journal entries made by Harry (or for that matter Tanisha). This means that errors made in journals are much less likely to be discovered before the entry is made.	Journal suggestions should be formally drafted with reasons for them and approval sought. This approval should be indicated by a signature and the journal documentation filed.
Access to the general ledger is given to under-qualified staff. Tanisha is the sales director making it unlikely that she holds an accounting qualification. Specifically, it is unlikely that the change to the provision for slow moving inventory could made correctly by someone without a thorough grasp of accounting rules. Errors could be made, deliberate or otherwise, in a crucial accounting document.	Access to the general ledger should be restricted to the FD and the CA only and this access should require password entry. Passwords should be a secret, changed regularly and sufficiently complicated to prevent guesswork being successful.
General ledger accounts can be created without authorisation. Dubious transactions could be hidden more easily in accounts created for the purpose.	The creation of general ledger accounts should only be possible by either the FD or the CA. In all cases when a general ledger account is created then the system should alert both the FD and CA that this has happened.
A change to accounting policy has been made without approval or indeed consultation. Accounting policies must be consistently applied and appropriate for the business. If changed then adjustments may be required in comparative figures and an explanation made in the financial statements	The board must approve changes to the accounting policy. Evidence for the need of such a change must be shown and the financial effect calculated.
The friendship between the FD and the CA could undermine the controls within the business. There is evidence of this already as the FD is not asking for sight of journals from the CA due to a "trusting" environment that exists between them.	The business would struggle to enforce a more business-like relationship at this stage (the friendship having been formed), consequently a third person should review all journals and jointly produced work. This might have to be an internal auditor or other person with the requisite accounting knowledge.

Section 4

MOCK ASSESSMENT QUESTIONS

TASK 1   **(20 marks)**

(a)   As well as selling via independent retailers and its website, Bonanza also has a shop at the factory. The general accounts clerk, Laura Wood, visits the shop at random without prior notification and does spot checks on the tills at the shop. She counts the cash in the till, adjusts for the initial float and reconciles this figure to the record of sales made from the till system that day.

Which of the following activities would be revealed by such a control? One mark for each correct answer.   **(4 marks)**

Forged bank notes had been accepted by the shop	Would be/ Would not be
A discount had been allowed for damaged packaging and so the sale had not been made at full price	Would be/ Would not be
Cash had been taken from the till to pay for a staff members car parking	Would be/ Would not be
A customer had not paid the full amount promising to come back later	Would be/ Would not be

(b)   Bonanza's factory shop has been underperforming and so the manager felt under pressure to improve performance. Having tried more legitimate tactics, in some desperation, he began to re-package customer returns and to sell them as new versions. This meant his revenue was higher and his shop showed a higher gross profit %.   **(4 marks)**

Which of the fundamental principles of ethical behaviour does this most threaten?

Confidentiality	
Professional behaviour and integrity	
Professional competence and due care	

What action should be taken? Tick all that apply.

The manager should be reminded of the ethical principles upon which the Bonanza business is built	
The manager should be fired for gross misconduct immediately	
Customers affected should be contacted and replacement toys provided	

(c)   Bonanza has been having problems with staff members using their own names as passwords and so it has decided to introduce new protocols for the password system.

To maintain the best control which of the following protocols should be introduced?

(2 marks)

All passwords must contain a capital letter	
All passwords must contain a number	
All passwords must be changed every quarter	
All of the above	

(d)   Laura Wood, the general ledger clerk, maintains a non-current asset register which records all assets owned, their cost and depreciation and is reconciled in total and by category to the general ledger balances each year. The register is used to calculate depreciation with the total amount then being transferred to the general ledger.

Which of the following errors would be revealed by the existence of the register and its year end reconciliation?

(4 marks)

A machine was bought during the year and was entered as plant in the general ledger. The non-current assets register recorded this asset as a fixture and fitting.	Would be/ Not be
Depreciation on the above asset was applied at the rate of 15% rather than the correct 20%.	Would be/ Not be
An asset was stolen during the year but this theft was not discovered until well after the year end.	Would be/ Not be
An asset was bought during the year which included a substantial charge for delivery. The delivery charge was debited to distribution costs in the general ledger but as part of the asset cost in the non-current asset register	Would be/ Not be

(e)   The employee involved in the above asset theft was eventually caught whilst trying to steal again (this time inventory), which he intended to sell at the local market. It is suspected that these thefts had become habitual and that the he had a market stall selling stolen toys most weeks.

(4 marks)

Which of the fundamental principles of ethical behaviour does this most threaten?

(2 marks)

Confidentiality	
Professional behaviour and integrity	
Professional competence and due care	

What action should be taken? Tick all that apply.

(2 marks)

The employee should sacked for gross misconduct	
The employee should be sent a written warning over his conduct	
The employee should verbally be reminded of his obligations and warned against further indiscretions	

(f)   Entry to the non-current asset register is protected by a password.

Which of the following passwords is the most secure?   (2 marks)

Register!	
Hutton	
123456	
Gnd5dge	

TASK 2   (15 marks)

Bonanza sets a budget each year for the factory costs. The directors feel that consistency is important and so they adopt a top down approach. The production director, Lech Polaski, along with other members of the senior management team, bases the budgets on past performance, an analysis of the general market conditions and the need of the business to grow and hence satisfy its owners. Once these budgets have been drafted they are sent to the individual managers within the factory and broken down into even monthly amounts to give monthly targets.

The factory is organised into different production lines making different toys. Each manager is responsible for the total costs of their production line, including apportioned overall factory overheads.

The remuneration of managers is as follows:

- Each manager earns a salary commensurate with the size of the production line managed, the number of staff they supervise and their experience to date.

- A bonus is possible if monthly costs incurred are less than that shown in the budget.

The managers are unhappy with this situation.

(a)   **Briefly explain why you think that the managers might be unhappy with the budget and rewards process outlined above.**   (6 marks)

Some of the managers are suggesting that the budgets be revised to take account of conditions that did not exist at the time of the original budget process being undertaken. Specifically the warehouse has experienced significant increases in business rates (a local tax) levied on them by the local council. Other managers have had to pay overtime to staff to cope with staff sickness.

(b)   Explain the general principles involved in the decision to revise a budget and then briefly discuss whether you would recommend a budget revision be granted in the above specific situations.

(9 marks)

General principles

Business rates increases

Overtime

TASK 3   **(15 marks)**

Bonanza does not have an IT director or even an IT manager, instead the finance director, Chris Burke, has looked after the IT infrastructure and it seems to run well.

Space in the head office is limited and Chris likes to keep an eye on things, consequently the main server is located in his office. This way, he reasons, no one can interfere with it without him seeing them.

The server is quite new and has the capacity to cope with expansion for a few years yet. It was quite expensive and of a good standard and that meant money was saved in avoiding the need for any back up machines or contract for the same. Data is backed up nightly using a Grandfather, Father, Son methodology. This means that three versions (generations) of the data is held at any one time.

Password setting is left up to the staff. Chris had a bad experience at his last employer when his boss forgot his password and it took a week to effectively hack into the system. "Passwords have to be memorable, since just like a house if you lose your key you can't get in" is his motto. The staff like this approach and chose names of their children or even their own names as passwords. This system is built on trust and the staff are expected not to disclose their passwords to third parties or other staff members.

The accounts payable system is a fairly standard one. Suppliers have an account, which is created by Jemma May (the accounts payable clerk) and payments are made on approved invoices monthly. Occasionally invoices go 'missing' and so Jemma processes copies sent by the supplier directly to her. If key suppliers refuse to supply (as they haven't been paid) then this can disrupt the supply chain and cause delays.

The sales side is centrally processed from orders sent by all the independent shops, which are collated together in batches of 20 shops and processed together. Robert Dobson (the accounts receivable clerk), checks that the batch header showing 20 shops (the size of the batch) ties in to the total after processing.

Use the answer spaces overleaf as follows:

- **Identify and explain five weaknesses from the above system description**

- **For each weakness briefly explain the effect it could have on the company**

Weakness	Effect of Weakness

TASK 4 (15 marks)

Due to market pressures, the Board of Bonanza are considering moving the existing factory to a cheaper location outside of London.

One possible location is under consideration. A staff member of Bonanza has considered the costs involved in a factory move but you have been asked to consider the approach and report back.

The staff member has produced the following schedule showing the various costs involved in the move:

Item	Notes	Cost included in the project appraisal
Research costs	Cost incurred to date in researching the existing and new cost structures of the two factories in question.	This has cost £2,000 to date including a valuation fee and director's time.
Rent	The existing factory is rented for £120,000 per annum. The lease comes to an end shortly and Bonanza will be able to exit.	This rent will be saved.
Staff costs	Existing Bonanza staff will be able to either move location to the new shop or take early retirement. Overall staff levels will fall by 20%	Those staff re-locating will cost £850,000 in employment costs. 20% of the £850,000 has been deducted as well.
Plant and equipment	The old production lines cannot be transferred, as the new factory is smaller. The new equipment will cost £800,000 and will have a useful economic life of 5 years.	Depreciation on old equipment will be saved of £40,000 per annum. £160,000 of extra depreciation per annum has been included for the new equipment.
Central allocated overhead	The new factory will be allocated with less overhead (as it is smaller)	Allocated overhead will be £120,000 per annum for the new factory

You have been asked to review this analysis using the principles of relevant costing to help ensure that the correct decision is made.

Use the answer spaces overleaf as follows:

- **Briefly explain the principles behind relevant cash flows for decision making.** **(3 marks)**

- **Comment on each of the costs above as to whether the costs included in the appraisal are correct.** **(10 marks)**

- **Suggest ONE cash flow type not included in the above table that should be considered in the project appraisal.** **(2 marks)**

(15 marks)

Relevant cash flow principles

Item	Comment on treatment
Research costs	
Rent	
Staff costs	

Item	Comment on treatment
Equipment	
Central allocated overhead	

Cash flows incorrectly excluded	
1	

TASK 5 (20 marks)

Bonanza uses performance measures in four areas or perspectives. These are shown in the background information but broadly are:

Perspective 1: Learning and training

Perspective 2: Internal business processes

Perspective 3: Customers

Perspective 4: Financial outlook

Data from the management information system is now provided, comparing the latest forecasts for 20X6 with actual figures for 20X5:

	Notes	20X6	20X5
Learning and training			
Staff retention rate		75%	85%
% Of staff on an apprenticeship		10%	15%
% Of staff attending service training		65%	75%
Staff wellbeing rating (out of 100)	1	55%	80%
Internal business processes			
Product returns rate – from shops		2%	2%
Product returns rate – from website sales		5%	5%
Customers			
Satisfaction of product			
Items bought via shops	2	98%	98%
Items bough through website	2	88%	90%
Number of deliveries/invoices		925,000	800,000
Complaints about late delivery		57,812	40,000
Complaints about incorrect invoicing		16,500	16,000
Complaints about incorrect goods delivered		27,750	20,000
Brand recognition	3	82%	85%
Financial outlook			
Gross profit%		43.2%	?%
Operating profit %		4.0%	?%
Inventory holding period		90 days	? days
Gearing (debt/total long term finance)	4	15.0%	?%

Notes:

1   This is assessed using a confidential staff questionnaire. The rating is a weighted index based on a variety of factors including the degree staff feel 'supported' and 'valued'.

2   This is assessed by customer survey.

3   This is assessed by external research.

4   Gearing is measured as debt/(debt +equity).

(a) Complete the financial ratio calculations missing from the table (to one decimal place only)　(4 marks)

Financial outlook	Notes	20X6	20X5
Gross profit%		43.2%	
Operating profit %		4.0%	
Inventory holding period		90 days	
Gearing		15.0%	

(b) With regard to complaints, which of the following statements is true?　(2 marks)

The rate of complaints is up in all categories	
Delivering on time is more important than delivering the right goods	
The overall complaint rate is up 1.5%	

(c) Provide an interpretation of the performance of the business with regard to 'learning and training', clearly explaining the consequences for the business as a result of the data. Also explain at TWO links between the data in the learning and training perspective with one other category of performance assessment within the balanced scorecard.　(14 marks)

TASK 6 (15 marks)

Bonanza's payroll system and overtime

Permanent employees in both the factory and the warehouse work a standard number of hours per week as specified in their employment contract. However, when the factory (or the warehouse) is busy, staff can be requested by management to work overtime. This can either be paid on a monthly basis or accrued and taken as days off.

Employees record any overtime worked and days taken off on weekly overtime sheets which are sent to the payroll department. The standard hours per employee are automatically set up in the system and the overtime sheets are entered by clerks into the payroll package, which automatically calculates the gross and net pay along with relevant deductions. These calculations are not checked at all. Wages are increased by the rate of inflation each year and the clerks are responsible for updating the standing data in the payroll system.

Employees are paid on a monthly basis by bank transfer for their contracted weekly hours and for any overtime worked in the previous month. If employees choose to be paid for overtime, authorisation is required by production or warehouse managers of any overtime in excess of 30% of standard hours. If employees choose instead to take days off, the payroll clerks should check back to the 'overtime worked' report; however, this report is not always checked.

The 'overtime worked' report, which details any overtime recorded by employees, is run by the payroll department weekly and emailed to department heads for authorisation. The payroll department asks department heads to only report if there are any errors recorded. Department heads are required to arrange for overtime sheets to be authorised by an alternative responsible official if they are away on annual leave; however, there are instances where this arrangement has not occurred.

The payroll package produces a list of payments per employee; this links into the bank system to produce a list of automatic payments. The finance director reviews the total list of bank transfers and compares this to the total amount to be paid per the payroll records; if any issues arise then the automatic bank transfer can be manually changed by the finance director.

Required:

In respect of the payroll system of Bonanza, identify and explain FIVE deficiencies and recommend a control to address each of these deficiencies.

Deficiencies	Controls

Deficiencies	Controls

Deficiencies	Controls

Section 5

ANSWERS TO MOCK ASSESSMENT QUESTIONS

TASK 1

(a) Which of the following activities would be revealed by such a control?

Forged bank notes had been accepted by a shop	Would be
A discount had been allowed for damaged packaging and so the sale had not been made at full price	Would not be
Cash had been taken from the till to pay for a staff members car parking	Would be
A customer had not paid the full amount promising to come back later	Would be

(b) Which of the fundamental principles of ethical behaviour does this most threaten?

Confidentiality	
Professional behaviour and integrity	✓
Professional competence and due care *There is no suggestion he doesn't know what he is doing!*	

What action should be taken? Tick all that apply.

The manager should be reminded of the ethical principles upon which the GPL business is built	✓
The manager should be fired for gross misconduct immediately *The manager cannot be dismissed immediately without following due process.*	
Customers affected should be contacted and replacement toys provided *If possible customers should be compensated if they received inferior goods*	✓

(c) To maintain the best control which of the following protocols should be introduced?

All passwords must contain a capital letter	
All passwords must contain a number	
All passwords must be changed every quarter	
All of the above	✓

(d)

A machine was bought during the year and was entered as plant in the general ledger. The non-current assets register recorded this asset as a fixture and fitting.	Would be: The reconciliation is by category
Depreciation on the above asset was applied at the rate of 15% rather than the correct 20%.	Would be: Given the detection above
An asset was stolen during the year but this theft was not discovered until well after the year end.	Would not be: Not at the year-end in any case
An asset was bought during the year which included a substantial charge for delivery. The delivery charge was debited to distribution costs in the general ledger but as part of the asset cost in the non-current asset register	Would be due to difference in total costs.

(e) **Which of the fundamental principles of ethical behaviour does this most threaten?**

Confidentiality	
Professional behaviour and integrity	✓
Professional competence and due care	

What action should be taken? Tick all that apply. **(2 marks)**

The employee should sacked for gross misconduct	✓
The employee should be sent a written warning over his conduct	
The employee should verbally be reminded of his obligations and warned against further indiscretions	

This is a serious offence warranting a gross misconduct dismissal

(f)

Register!	
Hutton	
123456	
Gnd5dge	✓

Generally, the more complicated the better, avoiding words, names and strings of any sort.

TASK 2

(a) | **Reasons for discontent could be as follows:**

No consultation. The managers may feel that they should be consulted about the level of budget set. These people are expected to manage their business areas but seem to be disregarded in the budget process

Level of difficulty of targets. It could be that the budget process has resulted in some difficult-to-achieve figures. If the targets are too difficult, then this could be de-motivating and indeed annoying, given that at least part of a manager's reward is based on the difference between actual figures and the budget.

Growth is presumed. The pre-seen information tells us that there has been a downturn in the global macro-economic environment in which the company operates and increased competition from the video games sector, so sales of some lines may decline rather than grow

Seasonal aspects seem to be ignored. The budget process simply splits the annual budget into equal monthly targets. Given Bonanza makes toys, it is highly likely that sales up to Christmas will be much higher than other times of the year. This will make it harder to hit budget in some months than others.

The budget is based on the past. The past is, generally, a poor indicator of the future. Just because something was possible in year one it doesn't mean it is possible in year two. Staffing might have changed or levels competition might have increased meaning different targets are needed.

Controllability

Factory-wide costs are not under the control of production line managers so should not be included in their performance appraisal.

(b) | **General principles**

A budget revision should only be allowed if the budget contains an error (or poor estimate) that is outside the control of the business or the person upon which the budget is assigned.

It is important not to allow budget revisions for factors within the control of the business or the person being performance assessed. The risk here is that poor performance will essentially be 'blamed' on poor budgeting rather than weak operational actions.

In general the objective here is to end up with a fair and reasonable target that will properly motivate staff and managers.

Business rates increases

The business rates cost is entirely outside the control of production line managers so should not be included in their budgets or used for appraisal.

As far as the overall budget for the factory, the issue is whether the factory has been expanded or refurbished, then one could argue that the finance director chose to do that and so the increased cost was within their control. In this case a budget revision could not be supported. Any variance that resulted could instead be explained to senior management. However, if the local council have merely decided to collect more tax, then this is outside the control of the business and so a budget revision should be allowed.

> **Overtime**
>
> Much depends here on who decided to authorise the overtime and why it was incurred.
>
> If the board or Production Director instructed the production line managers concerned to pay overtime to hit production targets, then it was not under the control of the production line manager and a budget revision might be justified.
>
> On the other hand, if the production line made this decision, then the extra cost was within their control and no revision should be allowed – they should be held accountable for the overspend.

TASK 3

Weakness and effect thereof:

Weakness	Effect of Weakness
The **server location** is poor. It is unlikely that a standard office is that secure and so when Chris is away the server is vulnerable. Equally a standard office might not be as fire protected or cooled, as a server room needs to be.	The server could be stolen (they are valuable) or otherwise damaged by fire or water. This could be accidental or deliberate. Equally access to it could be too free meaning that malicious software could be uploaded more easily than is desirable.
Back-ups of the programs themselves do not appear to be made nor does there appear to a replacement contract in place to replace a damaged server. (**Note:** The data backup system seems to be fine.)	In the event of damage the business could be disrupted for a longer period than in sensible. This could result in delayed processing of supplier payments or lost transactions as backlog occurs.
The **Password** system is poor. Leaving it up to staff to create passwords is risky, they will often take the line of least resistance creating easy to remember passwords rather than more secure versions.	Passwords could be guessed by 3rd parties or unauthorised other staff. This could mean data corruption or deliberate damage or even theft.
Copy invoices are sometimes processed on to the system. Only originals should be allowed.	Duplication could occur leading to duplicated payments. This also creates a culture that it is okay to bend the rules of the system, which could lead to other problems.
The **sales** data is processed in a cumbersome way, which presumably involves some manual reproduction of the data. Equally the batch header seems only to include a total for the number of invoices and no value total or other control totals (hash totals for example).	Data errors could be made which could mean the value of sales recorded does not tie in to what actually occurred.

TASK 4

Relevant cash flow principles

The principles behind the idea of relevant costing for decisions

When any decision is being made it can be difficult to determine exactly which figures should be incorporated and how significant they are. The principle behind relevant costing is that we only incorporate factors that are directly affected by the decision and to the extent that they are affected.

For an item to be included it should be:

- A future item: past costs and revenues are known as sunk and are ignored

- A cash flow: provisions, depreciations are not cash flow and should be excluded

- An incremental amount

    If, for example, we are comparing two possible outcomes:

    Cash position if we go ahead with the proposal   £A

    Cash position if we reject the proposal   £B

The relevant cash flow is the 'future incremental cash flow' and is the difference between the two outcomes = A − B

Comments of existing treatment:

Item	Comment on treatment
Research costs	These are sunk costs (past costs) and should be excluded from the appraisal.
Rent	The rent for the old factory will indeed be saved from the date the lease ends. When leases end there can also sometimes be extra payments to return the property to its original condition. These are called dilapidations and are relevant costs.
	However the new factory will presumably demand a rent payment and this should also be included.
Staff costs	The staff that relocate would have been paid anyway (in the old factory), so this cost is not relevant to the decision to move.
	Consequently the 20% calculation is also incorrect.
	Bonanza need to compare the wages before with the wages after the move to identify the relevant cash flow.
Equipment	Depreciation is not a cash flow and should be excluded.
	What is relevant here is the purchase cost of the new equipment (including installation) less the net realisable (i.e. scrap) value of the old fixtures if any.
Central allocated overhead	This is not relevant as there is no incremental cost at all.

	Cash flows incorrectly excluded (only ONE required)
1	The new equipment may result in other production cost savings that should be incorporated
2	The new equipment may result in higher quality, resulting in extra sales
3	Within staff costs it is hinted that some staff might take early redundancy. Redundancy payments will be relevant to the decision.
4	Given the change in location, there may be a change in distribution and transportation costs.

TASK 5

(a) **The ratios are as follows:**

Gross profit %:	28,126/62,000	= 45.4%
Operating profit %	2,570/62,000	= 4.1%
Inventory holding period:	(7,916/33,864) × 365	= 85 days
Gearing	2,168/(18,137 + 2,168)	= 10.7%

(b) **With regard to complaints, which of the following statements is true?**

The rate of complaints is up in all categories *The number of complaints is up in all categories but the **rate** of complaints with regard to incorrect invoicing is down slightly.*	
Delivering on time is more important than delivering the right goods *Delivering the wrong goods even on time is just as much a mistake.*	
The overall complaint rate is up 1.5% *This is correct: the complaint rate is now 11.0%* *(57,812 + 16,500 + 27,750)/925,000* *up from 9.5%* *(40,000 + 16,000 + 20,000)/800,000*	✓

(c)

Interpretation of performance of "learning and training"
The staff retention rate has fallen from 85% to 75%. Recruitment, development and retention of high quality staff are crucial to Bonanza's success, so this is a worrying trend. The implications for the business will include a loss of skills, additional recruitment and training costs, and an increased risk or errors and mistakes.
The lower % of staff undertaking apprenticeships is a result of forced cuts in apprenticeship training and, while resulting in cost savings are also likely to result in lower skills, reduced loyalty and lower job satisfaction.
Service based training has reduced by 10% points since 20X5 and this is perhaps unwise. This might indicate that the business has lost focus on the importance of service training. This is surprising giving the perceived weakness in this area in the pre-seen. The consequence of this is a reduced ability to 'service' the customers. Service is everything surrounding the product including delivery, invoicing and picking.

Customers are rarely happy if you deliver great product late, damaged or otherwise incorrectly and so this could result in lost sales in the future and a damaged reputation.

The above might explain the staff wellbeing figures. These are well down from 20X5 and perhaps poor levels of training might mean staff members feel a little 'unloved' by Bonanza.

Links to other categories on the balanced scorecard

A link could be made here to higher operating costs, as when staff members leave they will often have to be replaced particularly in this growing business. Recruitment costs can be significant; pushing up costs.

The link can be also made to the complaint rates. All the complaints issues seem to surround service levels. Late delivery and accuracy of delivery are up in percentage terms and in absolute terms. This is perhaps where the business needs to focus, with extra training on the importance of these areas given and stricter targets enforced.

Invoicing errors are not as serious as in 20X5 and not as prevalent overall but complacency must be guarded against here.

TASK 6

Deficiencies	Controls
The wages calculations are generated by the payroll system and there are no checks performed. Therefore, if system errors occur during the payroll processing, this would not be identified. This could result in wages being over or under calculated, leading to an additional payroll cost or loss of employee goodwill.	A senior member of the payroll team should recalculate the gross to net pay workings for a sample of employees and compare their results to the output from the payroll system. These calculations should be signed as approved before payments are made.
Annual wages increases are updated in the payroll system standing data by clerks. Payroll clerks are not senior enough to be making changes to standing data as they could make mistakes leading to incorrect payment of wages. In addition, if they can access standing data, they could make unauthorised changes.	Payroll clerks should not have access to standing data changes within the system. The annual wages increase should be performed by a senior member of the payroll department and this should be checked by another responsible official for errors.
Overtime worked by employees is not all authorised by the relevant department head, as only overtime in excess of 30% of standard hours requires authorisation. This increases the risk that employees will claim for overtime even though they did not work these additional hours resulting in additional payroll costs for GPL.	All overtime hours worked should be authorised by the relevant department head. This should be evidenced by signature on the employees' weekly overtime sheets.

Deficiencies	Controls
Time taken off as payment for overtime worked should be agreed by payroll clerks to the overtime worked report; however, this has not always occurred. Employees could be taking unauthorised leave if they take time off but have not worked the required overtime.	Payroll clerks should be reminded of the procedures to be undertaken when processing the overtime sheets. They should sign as evidence on the overtime sheets that they have agreed any time taken off to the relevant overtime report.
The overtime worked report is emailed to the department heads and they report by exception if there are any errors. If department heads are busy or do not receive the email and do not report to payroll on time, then it will be assumed that the overtime report is correct even though there may be errors. This could result in the payroll department making incorrect overtime payments.	All department heads should report to the payroll department on whether or not the overtime report is correct. The payroll department should follow up on any non-replies and not make payments until agreed by the department head.
Department heads are meant to arrange for annual leave cover so that overtime sheets are authorised on a timely basis; however, this has not always happened. If overtime sheets are authorised late, then this can lead to employee dissatisfaction as it will delay payment of the overtime worked.	Department heads should be reminded of the procedures with regards to annual leave and arrangement of suitable cover. During annual leave periods, payroll clerks should monitor that overtime sheets are being submitted by department heads on a timely basis and follow up any late sheets.
The finance director reviews the total list of bank transfers with the total to be paid per the payroll records. There could be employees omitted along with fictitious employees added to the payment listing, so that although the total payments list agrees to payroll totals, there could be fraudulent payments being made.	The finance director when authorising the payments should on a sample basis perform checks from payroll records to payment list and vice versa to confirm that payments are complete and only made to bona fide employees. The finance director should sign the payments list as evidence that he has undertaken these checks.